I0009437

Linux Programming for Beginners to Advanced

A Complete Handbook to Building, Debugging, and Deploying System-Level Applications

Beth Thompson

Copyright © 2025 by Beth Thompson

All rights reserved. No part of this book may be reproduced in any form or by any electronic or mechanical means, including information storage and retrieval systems, without written permission from the publisher, except for the use of brief quotations in a book review.

This book is a work of fiction. Any references to historical events, real people, or real places are used fictitiously. All other characters, organizations, and events portrayed in this novel are either products of the author's imagination or are used fictitiously.

Legal Notice:

This book is protected by copyright. This book is for personal use only. You may not distribute, sell, use or quote any part of this book without the permission of the author or publisher

TABLE OF CONTENTS

Introduction To Linux Development

Software development for the Linux operating system is known as Linux programming. Writing system software that communicates directly with the Linux kernel is included, as is creating graphical applications and command-line utilities. Developers, system administrators, and businesses all over the world choose Linux, an open-source operating system, because of its stability, security, and adaptability. Programmers have total control over Linux, unlike proprietary operating systems, which permits them to freely alter and distribute their software.

Anyone interested in cloud computing, embedded systems, software development, or cybersecurity must understand Linux programming. Because of the increasing need for Linux-based solutions, learning Linux programming can lead to opportunities in a variety of fields, including networking, artificial intelligence, and enterprise software.

A Brief Overview of Linux as an OS

Linus Torvalds first created Linux, an operating system that resembles Unix, in 1991. It is based on the Linux kernel. It adheres to the Unix philosophy of modularity and simplicity, in which small, effective programs coordinate to carry out complex tasks. Linux is an operating system that is open-source, which means that anyone can alter and distribute its source code without restriction, unlike Windows or macOS.

One of Linux's distinguishing characteristics is its compatibility with a wide range of hardware platforms, including embedded systems, supercomputers, mobile devices, and personal computers. Many environments, including servers, desktops, cloud platforms, and even Internet of Things devices, can use it because of its versatility.

Linux distributions, or distros, are variations of the Linux operating system that come with the Linux kernel, software packages, and system utilities. CentOS, Fedora, Arch Linux, Ubuntu, and Debian are popular distributions. Enterprise applications, embedded systems, security research, and general-purpose computing are just a few of the use cases for which each distribution is designed.

The Linux operating system's kernel, shell, system libraries, and utilities are its essential parts. The kernel manages resources like memory, CPU, and input/output functions, serving as a link between hardware and software. Users can interact with the system through the shell's command-line interface, and system libraries and utilities facilitate a range of administrative and programming tasks.

Multiuser and multitasking capabilities are two of Linux's main advantages. The system allows for the simultaneous operation of multiple users without interfering with one another's workflow. User and application access to files, directories, and system resources is regulated by the system's strong permission management.

Linux has many security features, including firewall support, permission-based access control, and regular security updates. Because it is open-source, the international developer community finds and fixes vulnerabilities fast. Linux is therefore a favored option for cloud computing, web servers, and mission-critical applications.

The Value of Linux in the Development Process

Modern software development in many different fields depends heavily on Linux. Linux is a popular choice for organizations and professional developers due to its flexibility, security, and performance. The system's adaptability to particular requirements makes it a perfect option for both development and implementation.

Linux is significant in development for a number of reasons, including the fact that servers and cloud computing use it extensively. Applications and services are hosted in Linux-based environments by major cloud providers like Microsoft Azure, Google Cloud, and Amazon Web Services (AWS). Linux is crucial for backend development and web hosting since it powers many web servers, such as those running Apache and Nginx.

Additionally, Android—the most popular mobile operating system worldwide—is built on top of Linux. Developing Android apps, embedded systems, or Internet of Things devices frequently requires developers to work with Linux-based environments. It is crucial to emerging technologies, as evidenced by its application in robotics, AI, and automotive systems.

Linux gives software developers access to a wide range of tools and a robust development environment. Numerous programming languages are supported by it, such as Python, Java, Go, C, C++, and Rust. Effective application development, testing, and deployment are made possible by the availability of open-source compilers, libraries, and frameworks.

Linux's open-source development is another factor that makes it worthwhile. Docker, Kubernetes, and Node.js are just a few of the well-known programming frameworks and projects that run on Linux. The cooperative character of open-source development promotes innovation, code reuse, and knowledge exchange. By participating in Linux-based projects, developers can hone their abilities and rise in the software industry.

When developing software, security and stability are crucial considerations, and Linux shines in both areas. Programmers can maximize security and performance with Linux's complete control over system configurations, unlike proprietary operating systems that might compel them to work in constrictive environments. Long-term projects and applications needing high uptime can benefit from its stability.

Resources for Linux Development

For effective Linux programming, a development environment that is well-equipped is necessary. Linux offers a multitude of tools that make software development, testing, debugging, and deployment easier. These tools include version control systems, debugging tools, text editors, and compilers.

An essential component of Linux programming are compilers. Numerous languages, including C, C++, and Fortran, are supported by the GNU Compiler Collection

(GCC), one of the most popular compilers. Clang is another well-liked compiler that is renowned for both its speed and suitability for contemporary development methodologies.

Writing code requires the use of integrated development environments (IDEs) and text editors. Linux programmers prefer Vim and Emacs because they are effective and customizable command-line editors. Sublime Text, JetBrains CLion, and Visual Studio Code are feature-rich coding environments with syntax highlighting, debugging tools, and version control integration for users who prefer graphical interfaces.

Debugging tools assist developers in finding and resolving code errors. Debugging C and C++ programs requires the use of the GNU Debugger (GDB), which enables programmers to examine runtime behavior, set breakpoints, and examine memory. Performance optimization, memory profiling, and leak detection are all made easier with Valgrind. When debugging complex applications, Strace and Ltrace assist in tracking system and library calls.

Software development requires version control, and the most popular version control system on Linux is called Git. Developers can effectively manage various project versions, work with teams, and keep track of code changes with Git. Repositories for Linux-based project storage and sharing are offered by hosting services such as GitHub, GitLab, and Bitbucket.

Package management systems make dependency management and software installation easier. Package managers used by various Linux distributions vary; for example, those based on Red Hat use YUM or DNF, while those based on Debian use APT. These tools guarantee that software packages can be installed, updated, and managed by developers with ease.

The process of gathering and overseeing software projects is made easier by build automation tools. In Linux environments, Make is a conventional build tool; however, CMake and Ninja provide more contemporary options for managing intricate build configurations. By automating software testing and deployment, continuous integration and deployment (CI/CD) tools like Jenkins and GitHub Actions increase the productivity of development.

When working on network applications, Linux programmers need networking tools. Tools like Netcat, Wireshark, and Tcpdump are useful for analyzing network traffic and resolving connectivity problems. With the help of Secure Shell (SSH), developers can safely access Linux servers from a distance and manage and launch applications.

The use of virtualization and containerization technologies, like Docker and Kubernetes, has transformed software deployment. By using these tools, developers can produce portable, lightweight application environments that function reliably on various cloud and Linux distributions. Testing and development are facilitated by the ability to run multiple operating systems on a single computer thanks to virtualization tools like VirtualBox and KVM.

For software development, Linux programming offers a stable, safe, and adaptable environment. Developers seeking to create scalable, effective, and secure applications continue to choose it because of its wide range of tools and open-source nature. Learning Linux programming is an important skill that leads to a variety of career options, whether you're working with system software, web apps, embedded systems, or cloud computing.

Linux System Architecture

Linux system architecture is based on a layered design that ensures modularity, efficiency, and security. It consists of different components that interact to manage hardware resources, run applications, and provide user-friendly interfaces. The core of this architecture is the Linux kernel, which serves as the bridge between software applications and the underlying hardware. Surrounding the kernel are various system libraries, utilities, and user-space applications that facilitate interaction with the operating system.

The architecture follows the traditional Unix philosophy of building small, independent components that work together through well-defined interfaces. This design makes Linux highly scalable and adaptable, allowing it to run on devices ranging from embedded systems to supercomputers. The key components of Linux system architecture include the kernel, user space, processes and threads, memory management, and the file system.

Kernel and User Space

The Linux operating system is divided into two main areas: kernel space and user space. This separation ensures that critical system operations are protected while allowing applications to run efficiently without interfering with the core functions of the operating system.

The kernel is the heart of the Linux system, responsible for managing hardware resources, handling system calls, and providing essential services such as process scheduling, memory management, and device communication. It operates in a privileged mode, meaning it has direct access to hardware components and can execute low-level instructions. The kernel is divided into different subsystems, including process management, memory management, file system management, device drivers, and networking.

User space is where applications and utilities run. It includes everything outside the kernel, such as command-line tools, graphical interfaces, and user applications. Programs in user space do not have direct access to hardware but must interact with the kernel through system calls. This separation enhances security and stability by preventing user applications from directly modifying critical system components.

System libraries act as intermediaries between user applications and the kernel. They provide functions that simplify application development by handling tasks such as input/output operations, memory allocation, and network communication. The GNU C Library (glibc) is one of the most important system libraries in Linux, offering standard functions for application programming.

Processes and Threads

A process is an instance of a running program. Every time a user or the system executes a program, a new process is created. Linux uses a process management system that allows multiple processes to run simultaneously, enabling multitasking. Each process has its own memory space, execution context, and system resources.

Linux processes can be categorized into foreground and background processes. Foreground processes are those initiated by the user and require input or interaction, while background processes run without direct user intervention. Some processes, known as daemons, run in the background to provide system services such as logging, networking, and job scheduling.

Each process in Linux has a unique process ID (PID), which helps the system keep track of running processes. The process table stores information about all active processes, including their states, priorities, and resource usage. The states of a process include running, sleeping, stopped, and zombie. The scheduler determines which process gets CPU time based on scheduling policies, ensuring fair resource allocation.

Threads are lightweight processes that share the same memory space but execute different tasks concurrently. Unlike processes, threads within the same process can communicate and share resources more efficiently. Linux supports multithreading through the POSIX threads (pthreads) library, allowing applications to execute multiple tasks in parallel. This is particularly useful in applications requiring high performance, such as web servers and scientific computing.

Interprocess communication (IPC) mechanisms enable processes to exchange data and synchronize execution. These mechanisms include pipes, message queues, shared memory, and signals. By using IPC, Linux ensures smooth coordination between processes while maintaining data integrity and security.

Memory Management

Memory management in Linux is responsible for allocating and managing system memory efficiently. The operating system must balance memory usage among different processes while preventing memory leaks and ensuring stability. Linux employs a virtual memory system that abstracts physical memory, allowing processes to use more memory than is physically available.

Virtual memory is divided into pages, which the kernel manages using a paging system. When a process needs more memory, the kernel allocates pages dynamically. If the system runs out of physical memory, it uses swap space, a designated area on the disk that acts as an extension of RAM. Although swapping helps manage memory shortages, excessive use of swap can slow down the system.

The kernel provides various memory allocation mechanisms, including dynamic memory allocation functions such as malloc and free. The slab allocator is a key memory management component that optimizes memory allocation for frequently used data structures, reducing fragmentation and improving performance.

Memory protection ensures that processes cannot access each other's memory space, preventing accidental corruption or security breaches. The kernel assigns different memory regions to processes, including the text segment (program code), data segment (initialized variables), heap (dynamic memory), and stack (function calls and local variables).

To enhance memory efficiency, Linux uses demand paging, where pages are loaded into memory only when needed. This reduces memory usage and speeds up application execution. Additionally, the kernel employs techniques such as copy-on-write (COW) to optimize memory usage in processes that share common data.

File System Structure

The Linux file system structure follows a hierarchical design, where all files and directories are organized in a single tree rooted at the root directory (/). Unlike Windows, which uses drive letters (C:, D:), Linux mounts all storage devices within this tree, ensuring a unified file system.

The file system consists of different directories with specific purposes. The root directory (/) serves as the base, containing essential system directories such as:

- bin - Stores essential binary executables for system commands
- sbin - Contains system administration commands requiring root privileges
- etc - Holds system configuration files
- home - Stores personal user directories
- var - Contains variable data such as logs and temporary files
- tmp - Provides temporary storage for applications and users
- usr - Houses user applications and libraries
- dev - Represents hardware devices as special files
- proc - Contains virtual files providing system and process information

Linux supports various file system types, including ext4 (the default for many distributions), XFS, Btrfs, and ZFS. Each file system type has unique features, such as journaling, which helps recover data in case of system crashes. Journaling file systems like ext4 and XFS maintain logs of file changes, ensuring consistency and preventing data loss.

File permissions and ownership are fundamental aspects of Linux security. Every file and directory has an associated owner, group, and permission settings. Permissions are represented using read, write, and execute flags for the owner, group, and others. Users can modify permissions using commands such as chmod and chown, ensuring proper access control.

Mounting and unmounting file systems allow Linux to manage external storage devices. The mount command attaches a file system to a directory, making it accessible, while the umount command detaches it when no longer needed. Linux also supports network file systems such as NFS and SMB, enabling file sharing between computers.

Symbolic links and hard links provide flexible ways to reference files. A symbolic link is similar to a shortcut, pointing to another file or directory, while a hard link creates an additional reference to the same file on disk. These features make file organization and access more efficient.

The Linux file system structure is designed for flexibility, security, and efficiency. By understanding its organization, users and developers can navigate the system effectively, manage files securely, and optimize storage performance.

Setting Up a Linux Development Environment

A well-configured development environment is essential for efficient Linux programming. Linux provides a robust and flexible platform for software development, supporting multiple programming languages, debugging tools, and version control systems. Whether developing system applications, web services, or embedded software, setting up the right tools and configurations ensures a seamless workflow.

A Linux development environment consists of the operating system, compilers, text editors, debugging tools, version control systems, and additional utilities for testing and automation. While many Linux distributions come preinstalled with essential development tools, configuring a tailored setup enhances productivity and optimizes performance.

Installing Linux for Development

Choosing the right Linux distribution is the first step in setting up a development environment. Popular distributions for developers include Ubuntu, Debian, Fedora, Arch Linux, and CentOS. Each distribution has unique features and package management systems, but all provide a stable and customizable development environment.

Ubuntu and Debian are widely used due to their extensive software repositories, ease of use, and long-term support (LTS) options. They use the Advanced Package Tool (APT) for managing software packages, allowing developers to install essential tools with simple commands. Fedora is a cutting-edge distribution with the latest software updates and is preferred by developers who want access to new technologies. Arch Linux is highly customizable, making it ideal for advanced users who want full control over their environment. CentOS and Rocky Linux are enterprise-grade distributions commonly used for server and cloud-based development.

The installation process involves downloading the ISO file of the chosen distribution and creating a bootable USB drive using tools such as Rufus, Balena Etcher, or the Linux command-line tool dd. The system can then be booted from the USB drive to install Linux. During installation, developers can partition the disk to allocate space for different directories, such as /home, /var, and /swap, ensuring efficient system management.

Setting up a development environment on Linux often involves installing additional drivers for graphics, networking, and peripherals. Many distributions automatically detect hardware and configure drivers, but users can manually install missing drivers using package managers or proprietary sources when necessary.

Once Linux is installed, updating the system is recommended to ensure that all packages are current and secure. Running commands like sudo apt update && sudo apt upgrade on Debian-based systems or sudo dnf update on Fedora ensures that the development environment starts with the latest software versions.

Essential Tools and Editors GCC Vim Emacs

The GNU Compiler Collection (GCC) is a fundamental tool for Linux development. It supports multiple programming languages, including C, C++, Fortran, and Go. GCC translates source code into machine code, allowing applications to run on different hardware architectures. Installing GCC on Debian-based systems is done with sudo apt install build-essential, while Fedora users can install it using sudo dnf install gcc. The Clang compiler is another popular alternative to GCC, known for its fast compilation and detailed error messages.

Text editors play a crucial role in writing and editing code. Linux provides a variety of text editors, ranging from command-line-based tools to graphical IDEs.

Vim is a powerful and highly configurable command-line editor preferred by many developers for its efficiency and extensibility. It supports syntax highlighting, code folding, and multiple editing modes. Developers can enhance Vim with plugins such as NERDTree for file navigation and ALE for real-time syntax checking. Vim is installed using sudo apt install vim or sudo dnf install vim, depending on the distribution.

Emacs is another popular text editor known for its flexibility and extensive customization. It includes built-in support for multiple programming languages, a powerful macro system, and integration with version control systems like Git. Emacs can be installed using sudo apt install emacs on Debian-based systems or sudo dnf install emacs on Fedora. Developers can extend Emacs with packages like company-mode for auto-completion and Magit for Git integration.

For developers who prefer graphical editors, Visual Studio Code and Sublime Text offer modern interfaces with advanced features such as integrated debugging, extensions, and Git support. These editors can be installed manually from their respective websites or through package managers like snap and flatpak.

Debugging Tools GDB Valgrind

Debugging is a critical part of software development, and Linux provides powerful tools to help developers identify and fix errors in their programs.

The GNU Debugger (GDB) is one of the most widely used debugging tools for Linux. It allows developers to inspect code execution, set breakpoints, and analyze memory usage. GDB supports debugging of C, C++, and other compiled languages. Developers can start debugging a program by running gdb ./program and using commands like run, break, and print to examine the execution flow. GDB can be installed using sudo apt install gdb or sudo dnf install gdb.

Valgrind is a memory profiling tool that helps detect memory leaks, uninitialized variables, and buffer overflows. It is particularly useful for debugging applications that deal with dynamic memory allocation. Running a program with Valgrind using valgrind --leak-check=full ./program provides detailed reports on memory issues, helping developers optimize performance and stability. Valgrind can be installed with sudo apt install valgrind or sudo dnf install valgrind.

Other debugging tools include strace for tracing system calls and ltrace for monitoring library function calls. These tools help developers analyze program execution at a low level, making them valuable for debugging complex applications.

Using Version Control Git

Version control is essential for managing code changes, collaborating with teams, and tracking project history. Git is the most widely used version control system in Linux, providing a distributed workflow that allows developers to work independently and merge changes seamlessly.

Installing Git is straightforward using package managers. On Debian-based systems, it can be installed with sudo apt install git, while Fedora users can use sudo dnf install git. After installation, configuring Git with user details ensures that commits are correctly attributed. This is done using the following commands:

git config --global user.name "Your Name"
git config --global user.email "your.email@example.com"

Creating a new Git repository is done with git init, which initializes a version-controlled directory. Developers can add files using git add filename and commit changes with git commit -m "Initial commit." Git tracks file modifications and allows developers to revert to previous versions if needed.

Remote repositories hosted on platforms like GitHub, GitLab, and Bitbucket enable collaboration and backup. Developers can push local changes to a remote repository using git push origin main and fetch updates with git pull. Branching allows multiple features to be developed simultaneously, with git branch new-feature creating a new branch and git checkout new-feature switching to it. Merging branches is done using git merge, combining changes into the main codebase.

Git also supports advanced features such as rebasing, stashing, and interactive rebasing, which help manage complex development workflows. Tools like Git GUI and GitKraken provide graphical interfaces for users who prefer visual interaction with Git repositories.

A well-configured Linux development environment streamlines the software development process, providing developers with the tools they need to write, test, debug, and manage code efficiently. By installing Linux, setting up essential tools, using powerful debugging utilities, and leveraging Git for version control, developers can build robust and scalable applications across various domains.

Basic Shell Programming

Shell programming is an essential skill for Linux users and developers, enabling automation, task execution, and system administration through scripts. A shell is a command-line interface that allows users to interact with the operating system, execute commands, and run scripts. Shell scripts are simple text files containing a sequence of commands that automate repetitive tasks, manage files, and configure system settings.

Linux supports various shell environments, including Bash (Bourne Again Shell), Zsh, Ksh, and Fish. Bash is the most widely used shell, offering powerful scripting capabilities, command substitution, and process control. Understanding shell scripting helps users streamline workflows, enhance productivity, and build efficient system automation tools.

Introduction to the Shell

The shell is an intermediary between the user and the operating system, processing commands and executing programs. It interprets user inputs, runs system utilities, and manages processes. The shell provides several built-in commands for file manipulation, process control, and text processing.

Common shell environments include:

- Bash (Bourne Again Shell) - The default shell in most Linux distributions, known for its scripting capabilities and compatibility with older Unix shells
- Zsh (Z Shell) - An extended shell with improved auto-completion, syntax highlighting, and customization options
- Ksh (KornShell) - A high-performance shell with advanced scripting features and compatibility with the Bourne shell
- Fish (Friendly Interactive Shell) - A user-friendly shell with syntax highlighting, suggestions, and a modern design

Users can determine the current shell by running echo $SHELL. Switching between shells is possible by executing the shell's name, such as zsh or ksh.

The shell executes commands in a sequence, reading user input and processing it line by line. It supports various operators, pipes, and redirection mechanisms to control input and output. Commands can be combined using semicolons (;) or executed conditionally using logical operators like && (AND) and || (OR).

Writing Shell Scripts

Shell scripts are executable text files containing a series of commands that run sequentially. They automate tasks such as system monitoring, file manipulation, and software installation. A basic shell script follows this structure:

1. Shebang (`#!`) - Specifies the interpreter used to execute the script
2. Commands - A sequence of shell commands to be executed

3. Comments ('#') - Lines explaining the script's functionality, ignored by the interpreter

To create a shell script, follow these steps:

1. Open a text editor and create a new file
2. Add the shebang line `#!/bin/bash` at the beginning
3. Write the desired shell commands
4. Save the file with a `.sh` extension (e.g., `script.sh`)
5. Make the script executable with `chmod +x script.sh`
6. Run the script using `./script.sh`

Example script:

```bash
#!/bin/bash
echo "Hello, World!"
```

Executing this script prints "Hello, World!" to the terminal. Scripts can include variables, user input, loops, and conditionals to enhance functionality.

Handling Arguments and Variables

Shell scripts use variables to store and manipulate data. Variables can be assigned values using the `=` operator without spaces:

```bash
#!/bin/bash
name="Alice"
echo "Hello, $name!"
```

Shell variables can be classified into:

1. User-defined variables - Created by the user and accessible within the script

2. Environment variables - System-defined variables available globally (e.g., `$HOME`, `$PATH`)

3. Positional parameters - Command-line arguments passed to the script (e.g., `$1`, `$2`, `$3`)

Scripts can accept command-line arguments, allowing dynamic input processing:

```bash
#!/bin/bash
echo "Script Name: $0"
echo "First Argument: $1"
echo "Second Argument: $2"
```

Executing `./script.sh Alice Bob` outputs:

```
```

Script Name: ./script.sh
First Argument: Alice
Second Argument: Bob
```

The `$#` variable stores the number of arguments passed, while `$@` and `$*` contain all arguments. Argument validation can be implemented using conditionals:

```bash
#!/bin/bash
if [ $# -eq 0 ]; then
    echo "No arguments provided"
    exit 1
fi
echo "Arguments received: $@"
```

Loops and Conditionals

Loops and conditionals enhance script flexibility by enabling decision-making and iteration.

Conditional Statements

The `if` statement executes commands based on conditions:

```bash
#!/bin/bash
```
```

```
num=10
if [ $num -gt 5 ]; then
    echo "Number is greater than 5"
else
    echo "Number is 5 or less"
fi
```

The `elif` keyword allows multiple conditions:

```bash
#!/bin/bash
num=15
if [ $num -lt 10 ]; then
    echo "Less than 10"
elif [ $num -eq 15 ]; then
    echo "Equal to 15"
else
    echo "Greater than 10 but not 15"
fi
```

The `case` statement simplifies multi-condition checking:

```bash
#!/bin/bash
day="Monday"
```

```bash
case $day in
    "Monday") echo "Start of the week";;
    "Friday") echo "Weekend is near";;
    *) echo "Another day";;
esac
```

Looping Structures

Loops execute commands repeatedly based on conditions.

For loop iterates over a list of values:

```bash
#!/bin/bash
for i in 1 2 3 4 5; do
    echo "Iteration: $i"
done
```

Using a range:

```bash
for i in {1..5}; do
    echo "Iteration: $i"
done
```

While loop runs until a condition is false:

```bash
#!/bin/bash
count=1
while [ $count -le 5 ]; do
    echo "Count: $count"
    ((count++))
done
```

Until loop executes until a condition becomes true:

```bash
#!/bin/bash
num=1
until [ $num -gt 5 ]; do
    echo "Number: $num"
    ((num++))
done
```

Loops and conditionals make shell scripts dynamic and interactive, enabling automation of repetitive tasks.

Text Processing Awk Sed Grep

Text processing is essential in shell scripting for analyzing logs, extracting data, and modifying files. Linux provides powerful tools such as `awk`, `sed`, and `grep` for efficient text manipulation.

Grep
`grep` searches for patterns in text files:

```bash
grep "error" logfile.txt
```

Using options:

- `-i` ignores case (`grep -i "error" logfile.txt`)
- `-v` excludes matching lines (`grep -v "success" logfile.txt`)
- `-c` counts occurrences (`grep -c "error" logfile.txt`)

Sed
`sed` (Stream Editor) modifies text based on patterns:

Replace text:

```bash
sed 's/old/new/g' file.txt
```

```
```

Delete lines:

```bash
sed '/pattern/d' file.txt
```

Insert text:

```bash
sed '2i New Line' file.txt
```

Awk

`awk` is used for text extraction and formatting:

```bash
awk '{print $1, $3}' file.txt
```

Print lines matching a condition:

```bash
```

```
awk '$2 > 50 {print $1, $2}' data.txt
```
```

Advanced scripts combine these tools to process and manipulate data efficiently.

Mastering shell programming enhances system administration, automation, and software development, making Linux scripting an invaluable skill.
```

System Calls and Libraries

System calls are the interface between user-space applications and the Linux kernel. They allow programs to request services from the operating system, such as file operations, process creation, and memory management. Without system calls, applications would not be able to interact with hardware, manage files, or execute processes.

In Linux, system calls serve as a bridge between high-level programming languages and the underlying system functionality. They are essential for tasks like reading and writing files, creating and managing processes, and allocating memory. System calls are invoked using wrapper functions in standard libraries like the GNU C Library (glibc), which provides easier access to low-level kernel services.

Introduction to System Calls

A system call is a request made by a user-space application to the kernel to perform a privileged operation. Since user-space applications do not have direct access to hardware or critical system resources, they must communicate with the kernel using system calls.

The process of executing a system call involves:

1. The application calls a library function (such as `open()` or `read()`)

2. The function issues a system call, triggering a software interrupt

3. The kernel switches from user mode to kernel mode to execute the request

4. The requested operation is performed by the kernel

5. The kernel returns control to the application along with the result

System calls are categorized into various types based on their functionality, including:

- File management system calls (`open`, `read`, `write`, `close`)

- Process control system calls(`fork`, `exec`, `wait`)

- Memory management system calls (`mmap`, `brk`, `malloc`, `free`)

- Inter-process communication (IPC) system calls** (`pipe`, `shmget`, `msgsnd`)

- Network system calls (`socket`, `bind`, `listen`, `accept`)

Developers can inspect available system calls using the `man` command (`man 2 syscall_name`) or listing all system calls with `man syscalls`.

File I/O System Calls open read write close

File input and output operations in Linux are performed using system calls that interact with the filesystem. Unlike high-level functions such as `fopen()` in the C standard library, system calls operate directly at the kernel level, providing fine-grained control over file handling.

Opening a File with open()

The `open()` system call is used to open a file and obtain a file descriptor. A file descriptor is a unique integer representing an open file in the system.

```c
#include <fcntl.h>
#include <sys/types.h>
#include <sys/stat.h>
#include <unistd.h>

int fd = open("example.txt", O_RDWR | O_CREAT, 0644);
```

- `O_RDWR` opens the file for reading and writing
- `O_CREAT` creates the file if it does not exist
- `0644` sets file permissions (read/write for the owner, read-only for others)
- If successful, `open()` returns a file descriptor; otherwise, it returns `-1`

Reading from a File with read()

The `read()` system call reads data from an open file into a buffer.

```c
#include <unistd.h>

char buffer[100];
```

```c
ssize_t bytes_read = read(fd, buffer, sizeof(buffer));
```

- `fd` is the file descriptor
- `buffer` stores the data read from the file
- `sizeof(buffer)` specifies the number of bytes to read
- `read()` returns the number of bytes actually read or `-1` on failure

Writing to a File with write()

The `write()` system call writes data from a buffer to a file.

```c
#include <unistd.h>

const char 'data = "Hello, Linux!";
ssize_t bytes_written = write(fd, data, strlen(data));
```

- `write()` returns the number of bytes successfully written

Closing a File with close()

Once a file is no longer needed, it should be closed using `close()` to free system resources.

```c
```

```
close(fd);
```
```

Closing a file ensures that all buffered data is flushed to disk, preventing data corruption or memory leaks.


## Process Management (fork, exec, wait)

Process management system calls allow programs to create, execute, and synchronize processes.

### Creating a New Process with fork()

The `fork()` system call creates a new child process that is an exact copy of the parent.

```c
#include <unistd.h>
#include <stdio.h>

int main() {
    pid_t pid = fork();
    if (pid == 0) {
        printf("Child process (PID: %d)\n", getpid());
    } else {
        printf("Parent process (PID: %d)\n", getpid());
    }
```
```

```
    return 0;
}
```
```

- `fork()` returns `0` in the child process and the child's PID in the parent process
- If `fork()` fails, it returns `-1`

## Executing a New Program with exec()

The `exec()` family of functions replaces the current process image with a new program.

```c
#include <unistd.h>

int main() {
    char 'args[] = {"/bin/ls", "-l", NULL};
    execvp(args[0], args);
    return 0;
}
```

- If `execvp()` is successful, the original program is replaced by `ls -l`
- If it fails, execution continues in the original program
```

Synchronizing Processes with wait()

The `wait()` system call pauses the parent process until the child process terminates.

```c
#include <sys/types.h>
#include <sys/wait.h>
#include <unistd.h>
#include <stdio.h>

int main() {
    pid_t pid = fork();
    if (pid == 0) {
        printf("Child process running\n");
    } else {
        wait(NULL);
        printf("Child process finished, parent resuming\n");
    }
    return 0;
}
```

- `wait(NULL)` blocks the parent until the child terminates

Memory Management (mmap, malloc, free)

Memory management system calls allocate and manage memory for processes.

Allocating Memory with mmap()

The `mmap()` system call maps files or anonymous memory into a process's address space.

```c
#include <sys/mman.h>
#include <fcntl.h>
#include <unistd.h>

int fd = open("file.txt", O_RDONLY);
void *addr = mmap(NULL, 4096, PROT_READ, MAP_PRIVATE, fd, 0);
```

- `PROT_READ` allows read-only access
- `MAP_PRIVATE` creates a private mapping
- `munmap(addr, 4096)` unmaps the allocated memory

Dynamic Memory Allocation with malloc() and free()

The `malloc()` function allocates memory dynamically, while `free()` releases it.

```c
#include <stdlib.h>

int 'arr = (int ')malloc(10 ' sizeof(int));
```

free(arr);

```
```

- `malloc()` returns a pointer to the allocated memory
- `free()` deallocates the memory to prevent leaks

Mastering system calls and libraries allows developers to build efficient, low-level applications that interact directly with the Linux kernel, enabling high-performance file handling, process control, and memory management.

Concurrency and Parallelism

Concurrency and parallelism are essential concepts in modern computing, particularly in systems programming and multi-threaded applications. Both aim to improve the efficiency and responsiveness of applications by enabling the execution of multiple tasks simultaneously. While related, these concepts have distinct characteristics and implementations.

Concurrency refers to the ability of a system to handle multiple tasks at once, even if these tasks are not necessarily executed at the same time. Concurrency involves structuring an application to allow multiple tasks to progress without interference. This can be achieved by switching between tasks so quickly that the user perceives them as running in parallel. However, concurrency doesn't require tasks to be physically executed simultaneously.

Parallelism, on the other hand, refers to executing multiple tasks at the same time, typically on different processors or cores. Parallelism is a specific form of concurrency where tasks are physically running concurrently on separate processing units. This requires hardware support for simultaneous execution and can result in significant performance gains for computationally intensive tasks.

Understanding Processes and Threads

In a typical operating system like Linux, tasks are managed through processes and threads.

Processes

A **process** is an instance of a running program. It is an independent unit of execution that contains its own memory space, code, data, and resources. The operating system creates a process for each program that runs and provides it with a unique Process ID (PID). Processes are isolated from each other, meaning that one process cannot directly access the memory of another process unless through inter-process communication (IPC) mechanisms like pipes or message queues.

Key characteristics of processes:

- They have separate memory spaces

- They require inter-process communication to share data

- They are scheduled by the operating system and may run concurrently or sequentially

- They are relatively heavy in terms of system resource usage

Threads

A **thread** is the smallest unit of execution within a process. A process can have one or more threads, all of which share the same memory space, code, and resources. Threads within the same process are often referred to as **lightweight** because they are more efficient in terms of system resources compared to processes. A thread can be thought of as a sub-process or a task that runs independently within the context of a larger process.

Key characteristics of threads:

- Threads share the same memory space and resources within a process

- Communication between threads is easier and faster than between processes

- Threads are scheduled by the operating system and can run concurrently

- They are lightweight and more efficient in terms of resource usage

Threads are typically used to handle smaller, independent tasks that can be executed concurrently. This allows developers to create more responsive applications that can perform multiple tasks at the same time without requiring the overhead of multiple processes.

Using Pthreads

The **POSIX threads** (Pthreads) library provides a standardized set of functions for creating and managing threads in C and C++ programs. Pthreads are used to implement concurrency and parallelism in applications that need to perform multiple tasks simultaneously. The Pthreads library is widely used in Linux for thread management and synchronization.

Creating Threads

To create a new thread, the `pthread_create()` function is used. This function takes the following parameters:

- A pointer to a `pthread_t` variable, which will hold the thread's identifier

- Thread attributes (optional, usually set to `NULL`)

- A function that the thread will execute

- A single argument passed to the thread function

Example:

```c
#include <pthread.h>
#include <stdio.h>

void *print_message(void *message) {
    printf("%s\n", (char *)message);
    return NULL;
}

int main() {
    pthread_t thread_id;
    char *message = "Hello from the thread!";

    pthread_create(&thread_id, NULL, print_message, (void *)message);
    pthread_join(thread_id, NULL);  // Wait for thread to finish

    return 0;
```

```
}
```

In this example, a new thread is created using `pthread_create()`, which prints a message. The `pthread_join()` function waits for the thread to complete before the main program exits.

Joining Threads

The `pthread_join()` function is used to wait for a thread to finish. It ensures that the main thread or other threads will not continue execution until the specified thread has completed its task.

Mutexes and Semaphores

Thread synchronization is critical in multi-threaded programming to avoid conflicts when multiple threads access shared resources simultaneously. Two commonly used synchronization mechanisms are **mutexes** and **semaphores**.

Mutexes

A **mutex** (short for mutual exclusion) is a synchronization primitive used to protect shared resources from being accessed by multiple threads simultaneously. When a thread locks a mutex, other threads attempting to lock the same mutex are blocked until it is unlocked. This prevents data races and ensures that only one thread can access a critical section of code at a time.

Example of using a mutex:

```
#include <pthread.h>
#include <stdio.h>
```

```
pthread_mutex_t mutex = PTHREAD_MUTEX_INITIALIZER;

void *critical_section(void *arg) {
    pthread_mutex_lock(&mutex);
    printf("Thread entering critical section\n");
    // Critical code here
    pthread_mutex_unlock(&mutex);
    return NULL;
}

int main() {
    pthread_t thread1, thread2;
    pthread_create(&thread1, NULL, critical_section, NULL);
    pthread_create(&thread2, NULL, critical_section, NULL);

    pthread_join(thread1, NULL);
    pthread_join(thread2, NULL);

    return 0;
}
```

In this example, the mutex ensures that the critical section is accessed by only one thread at a time.

Semaphores

A **semaphore** is a signaling mechanism that can be used to control access to a shared resource. Unlike mutexes, which allow only one thread to access a resource at a time, semaphores can allow multiple threads to access a resource concurrently, up to a specified limit. Semaphores maintain a counter that represents the number of available resources or the number of threads allowed to access a resource.

A binary semaphore (similar to a mutex) can be used for mutual exclusion, while a counting semaphore can manage a pool of resources.

Example of using a semaphore:

```
#include <pthread.h>
#include <semaphore.h>
#include <stdio.h>

sem_t sem;

void *task(void *arg) {
    sem_wait(&sem);  // Decrement the semaphore
    printf("Task started\n");
    sem_post(&sem);  // Increment the semaphore
    return NULL;
}

int main() {
    pthread_t thread1, thread2;
```

```
sem_init(&sem, 0, 1);  // Initialize semaphore with value 1 (binary semaphore)

pthread_create(&thread1, NULL, task, NULL);
pthread_create(&thread2, NULL, task, NULL);

pthread_join(thread1, NULL);
pthread_join(thread2, NULL);

sem_destroy(&sem);  // Destroy semaphore
return 0;
}
```

In this example, the semaphore is used to control access to the critical section, ensuring that only one thread can execute it at a time.

Thread Synchronization

Thread synchronization ensures that threads operate in a coordinated manner, especially when they share resources or data. In addition to mutexes and semaphores, other synchronization techniques include condition variables and barriers.

Condition Variables

A **condition variable** is used to block one or more threads until a particular condition is met. Threads can wait on a condition variable, and other threads can notify them when the condition changes.

Example of using a condition variable:

```c
#include <pthread.h>
#include <stdio.h>

pthread_mutex_t mutex = PTHREAD_MUTEX_INITIALIZER;
pthread_cond_t cond = PTHREAD_COND_INITIALIZER;
int shared_data = 0;

void *producer(void *arg) {
    pthread_mutex_lock(&mutex);
    shared_data = 1;
    pthread_cond_signal(&cond);  // Signal the consumer
    pthread_mutex_unlock(&mutex);
    return NULL;
}

void *consumer(void *arg) {
    pthread_mutex_lock(&mutex);
    while (shared_data == 0) {
        pthread_cond_wait(&cond, &mutex);  // Wait until shared_data is non-zero
    }
    printf("Consumer consumed data\n");
    pthread_mutex_unlock(&mutex);
    return NULL;
}

int main() {
    pthread_t thread1, thread2;
```

```
pthread_create(&thread1, NULL, producer, NULL);
pthread_create(&thread2, NULL, consumer, NULL);

pthread_join(thread1, NULL);
pthread_join(thread2, NULL);

return 0;
}
```

In this example, the consumer thread waits for the producer thread to signal that data is available.

Forking and Handling Multiple Processes

When it comes to handling multiple processes, Linux provides the `fork()` system call to create a new process, which can be used to run tasks concurrently. Each process has its own memory space and resources.

Forking a New Process

The `fork()` system call creates a child process, which is a copy of the parent process. The child process gets a unique PID and can execute code independently from the parent process.

Example of forking a new process:

```
#include <unistd.h>
#include <stdio.h>
```

```
int main() {
    pid_t pid = fork();

    if (pid == 0) {
        printf("Child process\n");
    } else {
        printf("Parent process\n");
    }

    return 0;
}
```

In this example, the `fork()` call creates a new process, and both the parent and child processes execute concurrently.

Understanding concurrency and parallelism is crucial for writing efficient and responsive programs in a multi-core environment. By using threads, synchronization primitives, and process management techniques like `fork()`, developers can build applications that leverage the full power of modern hardware.

File Systems and Storage

In Linux, the file system is the backbone for managing and organizing data stored on disk devices. It defines how files are named, stored, accessed, and managed on storage media like hard drives, SSDs, and network storage systems. The Linux file system has a robust and flexible architecture that supports many types of storage devices, from local disks to remote file systems accessed over the network.

A file system in Linux is not just a way to store files but a comprehensive structure that defines how data is organized, indexed, and retrieved. It plays a critical role in managing everything from basic file operations to advanced storage management tasks.

Linux File System Hierarchy

The Linux File System Hierarchy (also known as the Filesystem Hierarchy Standard or FHS) defines the directory structure and the placement of files in a Linux-based operating system. It provides a standard organization for the file system, allowing consistency across distributions and simplifying system administration and file management.

At the top of the Linux file system hierarchy is the root directory, represented by a forward slash (`/`). Everything on the system is located under this root directory. The general structure of the Linux file system looks like this:

- `/` (root directory): The top-level directory that contains all other directories and files in the system.

- `/bin`: Contains essential binary files (executables) that are needed for the system's basic functionality, such as `ls`, `cp`, and `cat`.

- `/etc`: Contains system-wide configuration files that are used to set system behavior, including network settings, user configurations, and service management files.

- `/home`: Contains personal directories for each user, such as `/home/user1` or `/home/user2`. Each user's files are stored here.

- `/lib`: Contains shared libraries and kernel modules required for system operation and running executables.

- `/var`: Contains variable data, such as logs, databases, and spool files. It is used by applications and services to store their runtime data.

- `/tmp`: A directory for temporary files, which can be cleared at boot or at regular intervals.

- `/mnt`: A temporary mount point for file systems, usually for manual mounting of external storage devices like USB drives or network shares.

- `/dev`: Contains device files, which represent physical or virtual devices on the system (e.g., `/dev/sda` for hard drives, `/dev/tty` for terminals).

- `/proc`: A virtual filesystem that provides information about running processes and system statistics. It is dynamic and provides real-time data on system processes and hardware.

- `/sys`: A virtual filesystem that provides information about kernel parameters and configurations. It is used for managing kernel and hardware settings.

- `/usr`: Contains user-related programs, libraries, and documentation. Subdirectories include `/usr/bin` for user commands and `/usr/lib` for shared libraries.

This hierarchy creates a logical structure where files are grouped into categories based on their type and function. The organization makes it easier to navigate and manage files, ensuring that the system remains consistent and maintainable.

Working with Files and Directories

Linux provides a rich set of tools and commands for working with files and directories. These tools allow users and administrators to create, modify, organize, and delete files and directories, as well as manipulate their content.

Creating Files and Directories

To create a new file in Linux, the `touch` command is commonly used. This command is primarily used to update the timestamp of an existing file or to create an empty file if it doesn't already exist.

```bash

touch myfile.txt

```

To create a directory, the `mkdir` command is used. You can specify the name of the new directory as an argument, and it will be created in the current working directory.

```bash

mkdir my_directory

```

You can also create nested directories in a single command by using the `-p` option, which will create any missing parent directories as needed.

```bash

mkdir -p my_directory/sub_directory

```

Navigating Directories

The `cd` command is used to change the current working directory. You can navigate to different directories by specifying their path.

```bash

cd /home/user1/Documents

```

You can use `cd ..` to move up one level in the directory hierarchy and `cd ~` to go directly to your home directory.

Listing Files and Directories

The `ls` command is used to list the files and directories in the current directory. Adding options can modify the output. For example, `ls -l` provides detailed information about files and directories, while `ls -a` shows hidden files (those starting with a dot).

```bash

ls -l

```

Copying, Moving, and Deleting Files

The `cp` command is used to copy files or directories.

```bash

cp source_file.txt destination_file.txt

```

The `mv` command is used to move or rename files and directories.

```bash

mv old_name.txt new_name.txt

```

The `rm` command is used to delete files. Use `rm -r` to delete directories recursively. Be cautious, as this operation cannot be undone.

```bash
rm myfile.txt
```

Filesystem Permissions and Ownership

In Linux, file permissions and ownership determine who can read, write, or execute files and directories. This system of access control is essential for maintaining security and ensuring that only authorized users can modify critical files.

File Ownership

Every file and directory in Linux has an owner and a group. The owner is typically the user who created the file, while the group is a set of users who are assigned access to the file. These are displayed with the `ls -l` command.

Example:

```bash
-rw-r--r-- 1 user1 staff 1234 Apr  4 10:15 myfile.txt
```

In this example:

- `user1` is the owner of the file

- `staff` is the group associated with the file

- The file has `rw` (read and write) permissions for the owner, and `r` (read) permissions for others

File Permissions

File permissions are divided into three categories:

- Read (`r`)**: Allows reading the contents of a file or listing the contents of a directory

- Write (`w`)**: Allows modifying the contents of a file or adding/removing files in a directory

- Execute (`x`)**: Allows executing a file as a program or script, or accessing a directory

These permissions are represented in three sets: one for the owner, one for the group, and one for others. Permissions are modified using the `chmod` command.

```bash
chmod u+x myfile.txt  # Add execute permission for the user

chmod g-w myfile.txt  # Remove write permission for the group
```

Changing Ownership

The `chown` command is used to change the owner and/or group of a file or directory.

```bash
chown user2:admin myfile.txt  # Change owner to user2 and group to admin
```

Advanced File I/O Operations

In addition to basic file manipulation, Linux provides advanced file input and output (I/O) operations that allow users to interact with files in more complex ways. These operations are typically used in system-level programming and applications that need to efficiently manage large amounts of data.

File Locking

Linux supports file locking mechanisms that allow processes to lock a file to prevent other processes from accessing or modifying it simultaneously. This is useful in multi-process environments where data consistency is important. The `flock` system call and `fcntl` system call can be used for file locking.

File Mapping

Memory-mapped files allow files to be mapped directly into a process's memory address space. This is done using the `mmap()` system call. Once a file is mapped into memory, it can be accessed like an array in memory, providing efficient random access to large files.

Example:

```c
void *map = mmap(NULL, length, PROT_READ | PROT_WRITE, MAP_SHARED, fd, 0);
```

This approach avoids traditional read and write operations, allowing for faster data processing.

Disk and Storage Management

Disk and storage management is crucial for system administrators to maintain the health and performance of a Linux system. Linux provides a variety of tools and techniques to manage storage devices, partitions, file systems, and disk usage.

Managing Storage Devices

Linux uses the `/dev` directory to represent storage devices. Devices are represented by files like `/dev/sda`, `/dev/sdb`, etc., for hard drives and `/dev/nvme0n1` for NVMe drives. These device files allow programs to interact with the hardware at a low level.

Partitioning and Formatting

Disk partitioning divides a storage device into logical sections, each of which can contain a separate file system. The `fdisk` and `parted` utilities allow users to create, delete, and modify partitions.

Once partitions are created, they need to be formatted with a file system, using tools like `mkfs` (e.g., `mkfs.ext4`, `mkfs.xfs`) to prepare the partition for storing files.

Mounting and Unmounting Filesystems

After a file system is created, it needs to be mounted so that it can be accessed. The `mount` command is used to attach a file system to a directory in the Linux file system hierarchy.

Example:

```bash
mount /dev/sda1 /mnt/mydrive
```

To unmount a file system, the `umount` command is used.

```bash
```

umount /mnt/mydrive

```
```

Disk Usage and Quotas

Linux provides tools like `df` and `du` for checking disk space usage. The `df` command displays the amount of disk space used and available on all mounted file systems. The `du` command reports the disk usage of specific files and directories.

Disk quotas can be set to limit the amount of disk space or the number of files a user or group can use. The `quota` command is used to manage these limits.

Understanding Linux file systems and storage management is essential for administrators and developers who need to work with large datasets, manage storage devices, and ensure data integrity. The Linux file system provides powerful tools for managing files, handling permissions, and optimizing disk usage.

Networking Programming

Networking programming in Linux is a fundamental skill for developers who want to build applications that communicate over networks. From basic client-server models to advanced multithreaded networking applications, Linux provides powerful tools and APIs to facilitate network programming. The core of Linux networking is built on the **Berkeley Sockets API**, which allows processes to establish communication channels over the internet or local networks.

Linux networking programming is essential for applications such as web servers, file-sharing systems, chat applications, real-time data processing, and remote system management. This section covers fundamental networking concepts, socket programming, and advanced techniques for building efficient networked applications.

Introduction to Sockets

Sockets are the primary interface between an application and the network. They allow processes to send and receive data across different machines or within the same system. A **socket** acts as an endpoint for communication, identified by a combination of an IP address and a port number.

Types of Sockets

- Stream Sockets (SOCK_STREAM): These sockets use the Transmission Control Protocol (TCP), providing reliable, connection-oriented communication. Data is guaranteed to be delivered in order, without loss or duplication.

- Datagram Sockets (SOCK_DGRAM): These sockets use the User Datagram Protocol (UDP), which is a connectionless protocol. It is faster than TCP but does not guarantee data delivery or order.

- Raw Sockets (SOCK_RAW): These sockets allow direct access to lower network layers, enabling advanced networking tasks like packet analysis and custom protocol implementation.

Creating a Socket

The `socket()` function is used to create a socket in Linux. The syntax is:

```c

int socket(int domain, int type, int protocol);

```

- `domain`: Specifies the communication domain (e.g., `AF_INET` for IPv4, `AF_INET6` for IPv6).

- `type`: Defines the type of socket (e.g., `SOCK_STREAM` for TCP, `SOCK_DGRAM` for UDP).

- `protocol`: Specifies the protocol to be used. Usually set to 0, allowing the system to choose the default protocol.

Example: Creating a TCP socket

```c
int sockfd = socket(AF_INET, SOCK_STREAM, 0);

if (sockfd == -1) {

    perror("Socket creation failed");

    exit(EXIT_FAILURE);

}
```

TCP and UDP Communication

TCP and UDP are the two primary protocols used in Linux network programming. Each has its own advantages and use cases.

TCP Communication

TCP (Transmission Control Protocol) provides a reliable, ordered, and error-checked data stream between processes. It requires establishing a connection before data transmission.

A basic TCP client-server communication involves:

1. The server creates a socket and binds it to an address and port.

2. The server listens for incoming connections and accepts them.

3. The client creates a socket and connects to the server.

4. Both the client and server send and receive data.

5. The connection is closed when communication is complete.

Example: Basic TCP Server

```c
#include <stdio.h>
```

```c
#include <stdlib.h>

#include <string.h>

#include <sys/socket.h>

#include <netinet/in.h>

#include <unistd.h>


#define PORT 8080


int main() {

    int server_fd, new_socket;

    struct sockaddr_in address;

    int addrlen = sizeof(address);

    char buffer[1024] = {0};


    server_fd = socket(AF_INET, SOCK_STREAM, 0);

    address.sin_family = AF_INET;

    address.sin_addr.s_addr = INADDR_ANY;

    address.sin_port = htons(PORT);
```

```c
    bind(server_fd, (struct sockaddr*)&address, sizeof(address));

    listen(server_fd, 3);


    printf("Waiting for a connection...\n");

    new_socket    =    accept(server_fd,    (struct    sockaddr*)&address,
(socklen_t*)&addrlen);


    read(new_socket, buffer, 1024);

    printf("Message received: %s\n", buffer);


    close(new_socket);

    close(server_fd);

    return 0;

}

```
```
```

UDP Communication

UDP (User Datagram Protocol) is a connectionless protocol that sends packets (datagrams) without establishing a connection. It is useful for applications that require low latency, such as real-time streaming or online gaming.

Example: UDP Server

```c
#include <stdio.h>

#include <stdlib.h>

#include <string.h>

#include <sys/socket.h>

#include <netinet/in.h>


#define PORT 8080


int main() {

    int sockfd;
```

```c
struct sockaddr_in server_addr, client_addr;

char buffer[1024];

socklen_t addr_len = sizeof(client_addr);


sockfd = socket(AF_INET, SOCK_DGRAM, 0);

server_addr.sin_family = AF_INET;

server_addr.sin_addr.s_addr = INADDR_ANY;

server_addr.sin_port = htons(PORT);


bind(sockfd, (struct sockaddr*)&server_addr, sizeof(server_addr));

printf("Waiting for messages...\n");


recvfrom(sockfd, buffer, 1024, 0, (struct sockaddr*)&client_addr, &addr_len);

printf("Received: %s\n", buffer);


close(sockfd);

return 0;
}
```

```
```

Client-Server Model

The client-server model is a fundamental design pattern in network programming. A server provides services, and a client requests them. The client connects to the server, sends a request, receives a response, and then disconnects.

- The server typically runs continuously, waiting for incoming connections.

- The client initiates communication by connecting to the server's IP address and port.

A simple client-server architecture can use TCP or UDP depending on the application's needs.

Multithreaded Servers

A multithreaded serve is a server that can handle multiple clients simultaneously. This is important for scalable network applications such as web servers, chat applications, and online multiplayer games.

In Linux, multithreading can be implemented using the **pthread** library.

Example: Multithreaded TCP Server

```c
#include <stdio.h>

#include <stdlib.h>

#include <string.h>

#include <pthread.h>

#include <unistd.h>

#include <arpa/inet.h>


#define PORT 8080


void *handle_client(void *socket_desc) {

    int sock = *(int*)socket_desc;

    char buffer[1024];
```

```c
    read(sock, buffer, 1024);

    printf("Client: %s\n", buffer);


    close(sock);

    free(socket_desc);

    return NULL;

}


int main() {

    int server_fd, client_fd;

    struct sockaddr_in server_addr, client_addr;

    socklen_t client_len = sizeof(client_addr);


    server_fd = socket(AF_INET, SOCK_STREAM, 0);

    server_addr.sin_family = AF_INET;

    server_addr.sin_addr.s_addr = INADDR_ANY;

    server_addr.sin_port = htons(PORT);
```

```c
bind(server_fd, (struct sockaddr*)&server_addr, sizeof(server_addr));

listen(server_fd, 5);


while (1) {

    client_fd = accept(server_fd, (struct sockaddr*)&client_addr, &client_len);

    pthread_t thread;

    int *new_sock = malloc(sizeof(int));

    *new_sock = client_fd;

    pthread_create(&thread, NULL, handle_client, (void*)new_sock);

}


close(server_fd);

return 0;

}
```
```
```

Advanced Networking with APIs

Linux provides advanced networking APIs for handling complex networking tasks such as:

- epoll(): Efficient event-based I/O for handling thousands of connections.

- select() and poll(): Multiplexing techniques for managing multiple sockets.

- ZeroMQ and MQTT: High-performance messaging and IoT communication.

- Libcurl: For handling HTTP requests in networking applications.

- Raw Sockets: For creating custom network protocols and packet sniffing.

Mastering Linux networking programming opens up opportunities in system programming, cloud computing, cybersecurity, and distributed systems. Understanding sockets, protocols, and concurrency models allows developers to build high-performance, scalable, and secure networked applications.

Interprocess Communication (IPC)

Interprocess Communication (IPC) is a fundamental concept in operating systems that allows processes to exchange data and synchronize their actions. IPC is essential for enabling cooperation between multiple processes that may be running independently and concurrently. Linux provides several mechanisms to implement IPC, each with specific use cases and advantages. These mechanisms are used to achieve synchronization, data sharing, and communication between processes.

There are several methods of IPC in Linux, including pipes, message queues, shared memory, semaphores, mutexes, and signals. Each of these methods is optimized for different types of inter-process interaction, and understanding their characteristics is crucial for designing efficient systems.

Pipes and FIFOs

Pipes are one of the simplest and most widely used forms of IPC. They provide a way for processes to communicate by sending data from one process to another in a unidirectional flow.

Pipes

A **pipe** is a temporary communication channel between two processes that allows one process to write data into the pipe and another process to read it. Pipes are typically used for communication between processes that have a parent-child relationship.

The `pipe()` system call is used to create a pipe. It returns two file descriptors: one for reading and the other for writing.

Example: Using a pipe

```c
#include <stdio.h>

#include <unistd.h>


int main() {

    int pipefd[2];

    char buffer[128];


    pipe(pipefd);


    if (fork() == 0) {

        // Child process: writing to pipe

        close(pipefd[0]);

        write(pipefd[1], "Hello from child", 17);

        close(pipefd[1]);

    } else {

        // Parent process: reading from pipe

        close(pipefd[1]);
```

```
    read(pipefd[0], buffer, sizeof(buffer));

    printf("Parent received: %s\n", buffer);

    close(pipefd[0]);

  }


  return 0;

}
```

In this example, the parent process writes to and reads from the pipe through two file descriptors, `pipefd[0]` for reading and `pipefd[1]` for writing. Pipes are suitable for communication between related processes, especially for simple one-way communication.

FIFOs

A **FIFO** (First In First Out), also known as a named pipe, is similar to an anonymous pipe but allows for communication between unrelated processes. FIFOs are created using the `mkfifo()` system call, and they behave just like regular files, but the data written to them is retrieved in the order it was written.

FIFOs provide a more flexible alternative to pipes because they can be accessed by different processes and even across different programs. They are represented as files in the filesystem and can be used for inter-process communication between non-related processes.

Example: Using a FIFO

```c
#include <stdio.h>

#include <fcntl.h>

#include <unistd.h>

int main() {

    int fd;

    char *fifo_name = "/tmp/myfifo";

    mkfifo(fifo_name, 0666);


    // Writing to FIFO

    fd = open(fifo_name, O_WRONLY);

    write(fd, "Message to FIFO", 16);

    close(fd);


    // Reading from FIFO

    fd = open(fifo_name, O_RDONLY);

    char buffer[128];
```

```
read(fd, buffer, sizeof(buffer));

printf("Received: %s\n", buffer);

close(fd);


return 0;

}
```

FIFOs provide a reliable way for processes to communicate asynchronously. They are widely used in scenarios where different applications or scripts need to pass data to each other.

Message Queues

Message queues are another form of IPC that allow processes to send and receive messages. Unlike pipes and FIFOs, message queues allow data to be transferred in discrete chunks (messages) rather than as a continuous stream.

A message queue allows for asynchronous communication between processes. Each message in the queue has a priority, and processes can read messages in the order of their priority. This can help manage complex workflows where different processes need to communicate with varying levels of urgency.

The msgget() system call is used to create or access a message queue, and msgsnd() and msgrcv() are used to send and receive messages, respectively.

Example: Using message queues

```c
#include <stdio.h>

#include <sys/ipc.h>

#include <sys/msg.h>

#include <string.h>


struct message {

    long msg_type;

    char msg_text[100];

};


int main() {

    key_t key = ftok("progfile", 65);

    int msgid = msgget(key, 0666 | IPC_CREAT);

    struct message msg;


    // Sending message

    msg.msg_type = 1;
```

```
strcpy(msg.msg_text, "Hello from message queue");

msgsnd(msgid, &msg, sizeof(msg), 0);


// Receiving message

msgrcv(msgid, &msg, sizeof(msg), 1, 0);

printf("Received: %s\n", msg.msg_text);


// Deleting message queue

msgctl(msgid, IPC_RMID, NULL);


return 0;
}
```

Message queues are suitable for applications that require non-blocking communication with priority or need to send larger amounts of data.

Shared Memory

Shared memory is a powerful IPC mechanism that allows multiple processes to access the same region of memory. Instead of copying data between processes, which can be inefficient, shared memory enables direct access to a common memory area.

A shared memory segment is created using the shmget() system call, and processes can map it into their address space using shmat() and detach it using shmdt(). Shared memory can be used for high-performance applications, especially when multiple processes need to share large amounts of data in real-time.

Example: Using shared memory

#include <stdio.h>

#include <sys/ipc.h>

#include <sys/shm.h>

#include <string.h>

int main() {

   key_t key = ftok("progfile", 65);

   int shmid = shmget(key, 1024, 0666 | IPC_CREAT);

   char *str = (char*) shmat(shmid, (void*)0, 0);

   // Writing to shared memory

   strcpy(str, "Hello from shared memory");

```
printf("Data written: %s\n", str);



// Detaching shared memory

shmdt(str);



// Removing shared memory segment

shmctl(shmid, IPC_RMID, NULL);



return 0;

}
```

Shared memory is often used in high-performance applications where the overhead of copying data between processes must be minimized.

Semaphores and Mutexes in IPC

Semaphores and mutexes are synchronization mechanisms used to coordinate access to shared resources in concurrent programming. While they are not communication mechanisms on their own, they are critical for ensuring data consistency when multiple processes or threads access shared memory or other resources.

Semaphores

A **semaphore** is an integer variable that is used to signal between processes or threads. Semaphores allow one process to signal another that a resource is available or that a certain condition has been met. Semaphores can be binary or counting.

In Linux, semaphores are typically used with shared memory for process synchronization. The `semget()`, `semop()`, and `semctl()` system calls are used to create and manage semaphores.

Example: Using a semaphore

```
#include <stdio.h>

#include <sys/ipc.h>

#include <sys/sem.h>


int main() {

    key_t key = ftok("progfile", 65);

    int semid = semget(key, 1, 0666 | IPC_CREAT);


    struct sembuf sb;

    sb.sem_num = 0;

    sb.sem_op = -1;  // Decrement the semaphore (wait)
```

```
    sb.sem_flg = 0;


    semop(semid, &sb, 1);  // Wait on the semaphore


    printf("Critical section access granted\n");


    sb.sem_op = 1;  // Increment the semaphore (signal)

    semop(semid, &sb, 1);  // Signal the semaphore


    return 0;

}
```

Mutexes

A **mutex** (short for mutual exclusion) is a synchronization object used to ensure that only one thread or process can access a critical section at a time. Unlike semaphores, which can be used for signaling and mutual exclusion, mutexes are generally used for protecting critical sections in multithreaded programs.

Linux provides the **pthread_mutex_t** type and related functions like `pthread_mutex_lock()`, `pthread_mutex_unlock()`, and `pthread_mutex_destroy()` for working with mutexes in multithreaded programs.

Signals and Signal Handlers

Signals are a form of asynchronous communication used to notify processes of events such as termination requests, external interrupts, or other signals from the operating system or other processes. A signal can interrupt a process and trigger a signal handler, a user-defined function to handle the signal appropriately.

Signals such as `SIGINT`, `SIGKILL`, and `SIGTERM` are predefined, while custom signals can be defined for specific applications. The `signal()` function is used to set up a signal handler.

Example: Using signals

```c
#include <stdio.h>

#include <stdlib.h>

#include <signal.h>


void signal_handler(int signal) {

    printf("Received signal %d\n", signal);

    exit(0);

}
```

```c
int main() {

    signal(SIGINT, signal_handler);  // Handle Ctrl+C (SIGINT)

    while (1) {

        printf("Running...\n");

        sleep(1);

    }

    return 0;

}
```

Signals are useful for interrupt-driven applications and for controlling processes. They can be used to handle events such as timeouts, user interruptions, or other system signals.

Process Management and Scheduling

Understanding how Linux handles processes is essential for any systems programmer or developer working on the platform. Process management in Linux involves the creation, execution, monitoring, and termination of processes. Scheduling is equally important—it determines how processes get CPU time and ensures fair and efficient use of system resources. This section delves into the inner workings of Linux process management and scheduling, from creation and signal handling to job control and background execution.

Process Creation and Management

A process is an instance of a running program, complete with its own memory space, file descriptors, and execution context. In Linux, new processes are typically created using the `fork()` system call, which duplicates the calling process. The child process is nearly identical to the parent and inherits most of its attributes.

For more sophisticated management, Linux provides `exec()` family functions, which replace the current process image with a new program. The typical sequence in many applications is to fork a child process and then use `exec()` in the child to run a different program.

Example of creating and replacing a process

```c
#include <stdio.h>

#include <unistd.h>


int main() {

    pid_t pid = fork();


    if (pid == 0) {

        // This is the child process

        execlp("/bin/ls", "ls", NULL);

    } else if (pid > 0) {

        // Parent process waits for the child to complete

        wait(NULL);

        printf("Child process finished\n");

    } else {
```

```
        perror("fork failed");

    }



    return 0;

}

```

Process attributes such as process ID (PID), parent process ID (PPID), and priority can be accessed through various system calls and tools like `getpid()`, `getppid()`, and `ps`.

Linux provides `/proc`, a virtual filesystem that holds process and system information in real time. Each running process has a directory under `/proc` named after its PID, offering access to command-line arguments, memory usage, file descriptors, and more.

Signals and Signal Handling

Signals are software interrupts that notify a process that an event has occurred. Signals are used for interprocess communication or to communicate with the operating system. For instance, `SIGINT` is sent when a user presses Ctrl+C, and `SIGTERM` is used to request a graceful termination of a process.

Signal handling in Linux allows processes to define custom responses to signals using the `signal()` or `sigaction()` functions.

Example of a signal handler

```c
#include <stdio.h>

#include <stdlib.h>

#include <signal.h>

#include <unistd.h>

void handle_sigint(int sig) {

    printf("Caught signal %d\n", sig);

    exit(1);

}
```

```
int main() {

    signal(SIGINT, handle_sigint);

    while (1) {

        printf("Running... Press Ctrl+C to send SIGINT\n");

        sleep(1);

    }

    return 0;

}
```
```

Using `sigaction()` is generally preferred over `signal()` because it provides more control and better portability across systems. You can use signal masks to block signals temporarily and manage their delivery order.

## Process Scheduling in Linux

Process scheduling is the activity of the Linux kernel that decides which process runs on the CPU at any given moment. The Linux scheduler aims to balance responsiveness and throughput. It uses scheduling policies and priorities to manage how processes share the CPU.
```

There are several scheduling policies in Linux

- SCHED_OTHER: the default time-sharing policy

- SCHED_FIFO: first-in, first-out real-time scheduling

- SCHED_RR: round-robin real-time scheduling

- SCHED_DEADLINE: deadline-based scheduling for real-time tasks

The `nice` and `renice` commands let users and administrators adjust the priority of processes, affecting how often they get CPU time. Lower nice values mean higher priority, and higher values mean lower priority.

The kernel uses a Completely Fair Scheduler (CFS) for normal tasks, which attempts to allocate CPU time proportionally based on the weight (priority) of each process. CFS ensures that no single process monopolizes the CPU.

To inspect process scheduling and priorities, tools like `top`, `htop`, and `ps -eo pid,pri,ni,cmd` are commonly used.

Daemon and Background Processes

A daemon is a long-running background process that performs specific tasks or provides services, such as system logging, scheduling jobs, or managing network connections. Daemons usually start during system boot and run silently in the background.

To turn a regular process into a daemon, developers typically perform the following steps

- Fork and exit the parent to run in the background

- Create a new session using `setsid()`

- Change the working directory to root (`/`)

- Redirect standard input, output, and error to `/dev/null`

- Close any inherited file descriptors

Example of a simple daemon

```c
```

```c
#include <stdio.h>

#include <stdlib.h>

#include <unistd.h>

#include <sys/types.h>


void create_daemon() {

    pid_t pid = fork();

    if (pid < 0) exit(EXIT_FAILURE);

    if (pid > 0) exit(EXIT_SUCCESS); // Parent exits


    setsid(); // Start a new session


    chdir("/"); // Change directory

    fclose(stdin); fclose(stdout); fclose(stderr); // Detach from terminal

}


int main() {

    create_daemon();
```

```
while (1) {

    // Daemon code here

    sleep(10);

  }

  return 0;

}
```

Background processes are more temporary and user-driven. In shell environments, you can run a command in the background using an ampersand (`&`) like this

```bash
$ ./my_script &
```

Use the `jobs`, `fg`, and `bg` commands to manage background tasks interactively.

Job Control and Process Groups

Job control is the ability of a shell to manage multiple processes, including foreground and background jobs. This is particularly important in interactive environments, where users want to pause, resume, or move jobs between the foreground and background.

Each process in Linux belongs to a process group. The process group ID (PGID) allows the shell or terminal to send signals to a group of related processes. This is useful for managing pipelines and multitasking jobs.

For example, when you press Ctrl+C in a shell, the signal is sent to all processes in the foreground process group.

Common job control commands include

- `jobs`: lists active background and suspended jobs

- `fg %n`: brings job `n` to the foreground

- `bg %n`: resumes job `n` in the background

- `kill %n`: sends a signal to job `n`

You can also use `kill -s SIGSTOP` and `kill -s SIGCONT` to suspend and resume processes programmatically.

Internally, the shell uses `setpgid()` and `tcsetpgrp()` system calls to manage process groups and terminal access, making job control an essential feature of Unix-like operating systems.

Understanding process management and scheduling is key to writing efficient and responsive applications on Linux. It allows developers to build systems that make intelligent use of CPU resources, handle user input effectively, and integrate smoothly with the multitasking features of the operating system.

Memory Management

Memory management is a critical component of any operating system, and Linux is no exception. It is responsible for efficiently managing system memory, ensuring that processes have the memory they need while also preventing them from interfering with each other. Linux uses a combination of hardware features and software techniques to handle memory allocation, protection, and optimization. The goal is to provide each process with the illusion of having access to its own dedicated memory while efficiently managing system-wide memory resources.

Virtual Memory in Linux

Virtual memory is a fundamental concept in modern operating systems, including Linux. It allows each process to believe it has exclusive access to a contiguous block of memory, while in reality, the operating system manages physical memory through a virtual memory system.

In Linux, virtual memory is implemented with the help of hardware support, such as the Memory Management Unit (MMU), which translates virtual addresses to physical addresses. Virtual memory provides a number of benefits

- Isolation: Each process operates in its own memory space, ensuring that processes cannot directly access each other's memory unless explicitly allowed (via interprocess communication mechanisms).

- Efficient use of memory: Virtual memory allows the operating system to run more processes than the available physical memory by using techniques like paging and swapping.

- Memory protection: Processes are protected from one another, ensuring that one process cannot corrupt another's memory space.

The virtual memory system works by dividing memory into pages, typically 4KB in size, which can be mapped to physical memory or stored in swap space. When a process accesses memory that is not currently in physical memory, a page fault occurs, triggering the operating system to load the required page from disk into RAM.

Memory Allocation Techniques

Linux employs several memory allocation techniques to manage both user space and kernel space memory. The primary techniques used in Linux are

1. Buddy System: The buddy system is a technique used by the kernel to manage physical memory efficiently. In this system, memory is divided into blocks of sizes that are powers of two. When a request for memory is made, the kernel tries to

allocate a block that is large enough to fulfill the request but not excessively large. If no exact match is found, the system may split larger blocks into two "buddies" (half the size of the original block). This approach reduces fragmentation by keeping memory blocks relatively uniform in size.

2. Slab Allocator: The slab allocator is used to manage the allocation of small objects, especially in the kernel. It improves performance by maintaining caches of frequently used objects, such as inode structures or file descriptors. The slab allocator divides memory into slabs, each containing multiple objects of the same type, and each slab is managed independently. This technique minimizes fragmentation and improves allocation speed.

3. Page Allocator: The page allocator is used to allocate and deallocate physical pages of memory, which are typically 4KB in size. The page allocator can request pages from the buddy system and also handle memory pages that are freed or released back into the system. It is crucial for managing memory at the lowest level, ensuring that the kernel can efficiently allocate physical pages as needed.

4. Kernel Memory Allocation: When the kernel needs to allocate memory, it typically uses a set of functions like `kmalloc()` and `kfree()`, which are analogous to the standard `malloc()` and `free()` functions in user space. However, kernel memory allocation is more complex because the kernel must manage physical memory and ensure that certain areas of memory are not used inappropriately (e.g., interrupt handling or page tables).

These memory allocation techniques ensure that Linux can efficiently manage system memory while minimizing fragmentation, providing fast allocation, and supporting large systems with multiple processes.

Memory-mapped I/O

Memory-mapped I/O (MMIO) is a mechanism that allows programs to interact with hardware devices using memory addresses. In Linux, this technique is frequently used to map device memory or memory-mapped files into the address space of a process. By mapping I/O devices directly into the virtual memory space, the CPU can access device memory just like any other memory, making it faster and easier to interact with hardware resources.

MMIO is often used in kernel modules or device drivers to interact with hardware like network interfaces, graphics cards, or storage devices. It is also used in systems where shared memory regions are mapped into multiple processes' address spaces to facilitate interprocess communication.

To use MMIO in user-space applications, Linux provides the `mmap()` system call, which maps a file or a device into the address space of the calling process. This mapping allows the process to read from and write to the file or device as if it were regular memory.

Example of using `mmap()` for memory-mapped I/O

```c
#include <stdio.h>

#include <fcntl.h>

#include <sys/mman.h>

#include <unistd.h>


#define MEM_SIZE 4096


int main() {

    int fd = open("/dev/mem", O_RDWR | O_SYNC);

    if (fd == -1) {

        perror("Failed to open /dev/mem");

        return 1;

    }
```

```c
    void *mapped_memory = mmap(NULL, MEM_SIZE, PROT_READ |
PROT_WRITE, MAP_SHARED, fd, 0);

    if (mapped_memory == MAP_FAILED) {

        perror("Failed to mmap");

        close(fd);

        return 1;

    }


    // Read and write from memory-mapped region

    *((unsigned int*)mapped_memory) = 42;

    printf("Memory-mapped value: %u\n", *((unsigned int*)mapped_memory));


    // Clean up

    munmap(mapped_memory, MEM_SIZE);

    close(fd);

    return 0;

}
```
```
```

In this example, `/dev/mem` represents the physical memory of the system, and `mmap()` is used to map it into the process's address space, allowing direct read and write access.

Paging and Segmentation

Paging and segmentation are two different methods of dividing memory to manage virtual and physical memory effectively. Linux primarily uses paging for memory management, but it also incorporates elements of segmentation for certain specialized tasks.

Paging

Paging is the technique by which the virtual memory space is divided into fixed-size blocks called pages, typically 4KB in size. The physical memory is similarly divided into page-sized blocks called frames. When a process accesses memory, the operating system uses a page table to map virtual addresses to physical addresses.

If the required page is not currently in physical memory, a page fault occurs, and the kernel brings the page into RAM from swap space or disk. The use of paging allows the system to use more memory than is physically available, as pages can be swapped in and out of memory dynamically.

The Linux kernel uses a page table to store the mappings of virtual addresses to physical addresses. Each process has its own page table, and the kernel maintains a global page table for kernel memory. The page table structure is hierarchical, using multiple levels to manage the mappings efficiently. In modern systems, Linux often uses **64-bit page tables** with a large number of entries.

Segmentation

Segmentation, on the other hand, is an older memory management technique in which memory is divided into variable-sized segments, such as code, data, and stack segments. While segmentation is not extensively used for general memory management in Linux, it still plays a role in certain specific areas like the management of process address spaces.

In Linux, segmentation is primarily used in conjunction with paging to create efficient memory models. Segmentation allows the operating system to provide a clear separation between different types of memory, such as stack and heap, and provides a way to implement protection between different segments. However, paging is more efficient and flexible for managing general process memory.

Cache Management

Cache management is an important aspect of memory management, as it ensures that frequently accessed data can be retrieved quickly, reducing the need for expensive memory accesses to slower storage. In Linux, the operating system manages multiple levels of cache, including the CPU cache, disk cache, and memory cache.

CPU Cache

Modern CPUs use multiple levels of cache (L1, L2, L3) to store frequently used data. The Linux kernel does not directly manage the CPU cache but interacts with it via the Memory Management Unit (MMU), which handles the translation between virtual and physical addresses.

The kernel's memory management system works in tandem with hardware prefetching, which tries to anticipate which memory locations will be accessed next and loads them into the cache in advance. This increases overall system performance by reducing the number of cache misses.

Disk Cache

Disk caching is another vital area where Linux optimizes access to storage devices. When data is read from a disk, it is cached in the kernel's page cache. If the same data is requested again, it can be served from the cache instead of being read from disk. This significantly speeds up file I/O operations.

Linux uses the **buffer cache** and **page cache** to manage disk-based data. The buffer cache stores metadata, such as file system structures, while the page cache stores the contents of actual files. The kernel automatically handles the flushing of dirty pages (modified pages) back to the disk to ensure data consistency.

Memory Cache (Slab Caches)

In addition to disk and CPU caches, Linux uses memory caches for efficient allocation of objects in kernel space. The **slab allocator** (which was discussed earlier) is one such cache management system that provides a way to store frequently used objects in slabs. It reduces allocation time and helps minimize fragmentation in kernel memory.

By efficiently managing cache at various levels, Linux ensures that memory is used effectively, improving system performance and responsiveness.

Memory management in Linux is a complex and highly optimized system that makes use of advanced techniques like virtual memory, paging, memory-mapped I/O, and cache management to ensure efficient and secure memory use. By leveraging hardware features and sophisticated software algorithms, Linux provides a robust environment for both user-space and kernel-space memory allocation. Understanding these memory management mechanisms is essential for developers looking to optimize their applications and ensure that their systems run efficiently and securely.

Linux Security and Permissions

Linux, being a multi-user, multi-tasking operating system, places a significant emphasis on security to protect its resources, data, and users. The operating system is designed with built-in features that allow administrators and users to control access to files, processes, and devices. Linux security mechanisms are robust and flexible, offering several layers of defense, including file permissions, access control, user management, and application security. This section provides an in-depth look into these features, focusing on file permissions, user and group management, application security, and advanced security models like SELinux and AppArmor.

File Permissions and Access Control

File permissions are one of the foundational elements of security in Linux. Every file and directory on a Linux system has associated permissions that determine who can read, write, or execute it. These permissions are set for the file owner, group members, and others, providing a granular level of control over who can access and manipulate files.

Understanding File Permissions

Each file or directory has three basic types of permissions

- **Read (r)**: Permission to open and read the contents of the file.

- **Write (w)**: Permission to modify the contents of the file.

- **Execute (x)**: Permission to execute the file as a program (or to access a directory).

Permissions are divided into three categories

- **Owner**: The user who owns the file or directory.

- **Group**: Users who are members of the group assigned to the file.

- **Others**: All other users who are not the owner or in the file's group.

The `ls -l` command is used to display file permissions in a human-readable format

-rwxr-xr--

Here, the first character represents the file type, followed by nine characters representing permissions for the owner, group, and others. Each set of three characters corresponds to read, write, and execute permissions, respectively.

To modify file permissions, the chmod command is used. For example, to grant the owner read, write, and execute permissions, and the group and others only read permission, you can use

chmod 744 filename

You can also set file ownership using the chown command to change the file's owner and group

chown owner:group filename

Additionally, chgrp can be used to change the group associated with a file

chgrp groupname filename

Access Control Lists (ACLs)

For more fine-grained access control, Linux supports **Access Control Lists (ACLs)**. ACLs allow users to define permissions for specific users or groups beyond the basic owner/group/others model. ACLs provide flexibility by enabling multiple users and groups to have different levels of access to the same file or directory.

To view the ACL of a file, use the getfacl command

getfacl filename

To set an ACL for a file, you can use the setfacl command

setfacl -m u:username:rwx filename

This command grants the specified user `username` read, write, and execute permissions on the file.

User and Group Management

User and group management is a critical part of maintaining security in Linux. By controlling which users can access the system and what actions they can perform, administrators can ensure that resources are protected and that only authorized individuals can access sensitive data.

User Management

Users are the individuals or accounts that interact with the Linux system. Each user has a unique username and associated user ID (UID). In addition to the username and UID, users also have associated information such as their home directory, login shell, and group memberships.

To create a new user, the `useradd` command is used

useradd username

This creates a new user with default settings. You can specify additional options, such as the user's home directory and shell

useradd -m -s /bin/bash username

To set or modify a user's password, the `passwd` command is used passwd username

To view information about a user, you can use the `id` command, which displays the user's UID, primary GID, and group memberships

id username

Group Management

Groups in Linux are used to manage sets of users. Groups allow users to be grouped together for easier permission management. Each user can belong to multiple groups, and each group has a unique group ID (GID).

To create a new group, the `groupadd` command is used

groupadd groupname

Users can be added to a group using the `usermod` command

usermod -aG groupname username

To remove a user from a group, use the `gpasswd` command

gpasswd -d username groupname

Securing Applications

Securing applications is an essential aspect of Linux security. Linux provides various tools and practices to secure the applications running on the system, from securing network services to preventing unauthorized access to applications.

Security Best Practices

1. **Patch Management**: Keep your system and software up-to-date by regularly applying security patches. Package managers like `apt`, `yum`, or `dnf` make it easy to update installed software and libraries.

2. **Minimize the Attack Surface**: Avoid running unnecessary services or applications. By disabling unused services, you reduce the number of potential entry points for attackers.

3. **Least Privilege Principle**: Always run applications with the least amount of privileges necessary. For example, instead of running an application as the root user, consider creating a dedicated user with only the permissions required for the application to function.

4. **Secure Configuration**: Applications should be configured securely. This includes disabling unnecessary features, using strong authentication methods, and configuring encryption for sensitive data.

Application Sandboxing

Sandboxing is a technique used to isolate applications and limit their access to system resources. Linux provides tools like **seccomp** and **AppArmor** to apply sandboxing to applications, restricting what system calls and resources they can access.

The **AppArmor** security module restricts the actions that processes can perform, using security profiles that define what resources an application can access. Profiles are applied to specific applications to enforce policies for file access, network access, and other system resources.

The **seccomp** mechanism allows for more fine-grained control over the system calls that applications can invoke. Seccomp restricts an application to a predefined set of system calls, limiting the potential attack surface if the application is compromised.

SELinux and AppArmor

Linux provides two major Mandatory Access Control (MAC) systems to enhance the security of applications and processes: **SELinux** and **AppArmor**.

SELinux

Security-Enhanced Linux (SELinux) is a Linux kernel security module that provides a framework for enforcing access control policies. SELinux is designed to protect against unauthorized access and modification of sensitive data by enforcing strict policies on how processes interact with each other and with system resources.

SELinux operates by labeling files, processes, and other resources with security contexts, which are then used to determine whether a given action is allowed. These contexts define which processes are allowed to read, write, or execute specific files, ensuring that even if an attacker gains access to a system, their ability to perform malicious actions is limited.

The `getenforce` command is used to check the current status of SELinux

getenforce

To change the SELinux mode, the `setenforce` command is used

setenforce 0   # Disable SELinux enforcement

setenforce 1   # Enable SELinux enforcement

You can configure SELinux policies using tools like `semanage` and `setsebool` to define rules for specific applications and processes.

AppArmor

AppArmor is another MAC system that provides application-level security by enforcing security profiles. Unlike SELinux, which is based on labeling and complex policy rules, AppArmor profiles are path-based, making it easier to configure and maintain.

AppArmor works by restricting applications to a set of resources defined in its security profile. If an application tries to access resources outside of its allowed set, AppArmor blocks the action and logs the event.

You can check the status of AppArmor with the `aa-status` command

aa-status

To enforce a specific profile, use

aa-enforce /path/to/application

To disable a profile, use

aa-disable /path/to/application

Encryption and Secure Communication

Encryption is a fundamental security tool used to protect data at rest and in transit. Linux offers several mechanisms for encryption and secure communication.

Disk Encryption

Linux supports full disk encryption (FDE) using tools like **LUKS (Linux Unified Key Setup)**. LUKS provides strong encryption for disk partitions and ensures that data cannot be accessed without the appropriate decryption key.

To set up LUKS encryption on a device, you can use the `cryptsetup` command

cryptsetup luksFormat /dev/sdX

Secure Communication

For secure communication over the network, Linux provides tools like **SSH (Secure Shell)** for remote access and **TLS/SSL** for securing network services. SSH allows secure remote login and file transfer over an insecure network.

To encrypt communication with SSL/TLS, Linux offers libraries like **OpenSSL** and utilities like **stunnel** for wrapping unencrypted protocols (e.g., HTTP) with SSL/TLS encryption.

File Encryption

To encrypt individual files, Linux offers tools like **GPG (GNU Privacy Guard)**. GPG can encrypt files with public keys and allow for secure sharing of encrypted content.

Example of encrypting a file with GPG

```
gpg -c filename
```

This command prompts for a passphrase to encrypt the file.

Linux security is a broad and complex field, encompassing various tools, mechanisms, and best practices to ensure the integrity and confidentiality of system resources. By understanding and applying concepts like file permissions, user and group management, application security, SELinux and AppArmor, and encryption, administrators and users can significantly enhance the security of their Linux systems and protect them against threats. Properly securing a Linux system requires a comprehensive approach that involves securing files, processes, and communications, as well as staying informed about evolving security practices.

Advanced Linux Programming Concepts

Linux programming is vast and intricate, offering a wide range of advanced concepts that allow developers to leverage the full power of the operating system. From system performance tuning to network protocols and kernel-level programming, mastering these advanced concepts enables developers to optimize their applications, create custom kernel modules, and troubleshoot performance bottlenecks efficiently. This section covers system performance tuning, kernel modules, shared libraries, network protocols, and advanced debugging techniques, all of which are essential skills for experienced Linux programmers.

System Performance Tuning

Performance tuning is a crucial aspect of Linux programming, as it helps ensure that a system operates efficiently, even under heavy loads. Linux provides various tools and techniques to identify and resolve performance issues, such as CPU bottlenecks, memory problems, and disk I/O contention.

CPU and Process Scheduling

The Linux kernel uses a sophisticated scheduler to allocate CPU time to processes. The scheduler makes decisions based on various factors, such as process priority, CPU affinity, and the number of available processors. To optimize CPU usage, developers need to understand how the Linux scheduler works and adjust system parameters accordingly.

- nice: The `nice` command allows a user to change the priority of a process. The higher the nice value, the lower the process priority. This is useful when running background processes that should not interfere with more important tasks.

```bash
nice -n 10 command
```

- cpuset: CPU affinity refers to binding processes to specific CPUs. This can be useful for performance tuning in multi-core systems where certain tasks can benefit from running on specific processors. The `taskset` command is used to set CPU affinity for a process.

```bash
taskset -c 0,1 command
```

Memory Tuning

Memory management in Linux is handled through various subsystems, such as the page cache, swap space, and buffer cache. Efficient memory management is crucial for performance, especially in systems with limited RAM or heavy workloads.

- vmstat: The `vmstat` command provides detailed statistics about virtual memory usage, including information on page faults, swap activity, and memory paging. By monitoring these metrics, you can identify when the system is under memory pressure.

```bash
vmstat 1
```

- swappiness: The `swappiness` parameter controls the kernel's tendency to swap memory pages to disk. Lower values prioritize keeping pages in memory, while higher values encourage swapping. You can adjust this value dynamically to fine-tune memory management for your workload.

```bash
sysctl vm.swappiness=10
```

Disk I/O and Filesystem Tuning

Disk I/O is another critical aspect of system performance. When working with high-performance applications or large datasets, it's important to monitor disk usage and optimize filesystem settings.

- iostat: The `iostat` command provides information about CPU utilization and disk I/O. It helps you identify disks that are underperforming or have high read/write latency.

```bash
```

```
iostat -x 1
```

- tune2fs: For ext2/3/4 filesystems, the `tune2fs` command allows you to adjust filesystem parameters, such as block size, inodes, and reserved blocks, to optimize performance.

```bash
tune2fs -o journal_data_writeback /dev/sda1
```

Network Performance Tuning

Network performance is often a bottleneck in distributed applications or web services. Linux provides several mechanisms for tuning network performance, including adjusting buffer sizes, TCP parameters, and packet filtering settings.

- sysctl: Many network parameters, such as TCP buffer sizes, can be adjusted using `sysctl`. For example, you can increase the size of the send and receive buffers for TCP connections to improve network throughput.

```bash

sysctl -w net.core.rmem_max=16777216

sysctl -w net.core.wmem_max=16777216

```

- ethtool: `ethtool` is a powerful command-line tool for querying and controlling network interface settings. You can use it to configure network interface parameters, such as speed, duplex mode, and offloading features.

```bash

ethtool -s eth0 speed 1000 duplex full

```

Kernel Modules and Drivers

Kernel modules are essential components of the Linux kernel that allow the operating system to extend its functionality without requiring a reboot. Modules can provide support for new hardware devices, file systems, or network protocols. Writing kernel modules and understanding kernel-level programming is a critical skill for advanced Linux programmers.

Writing Kernel Modules

A kernel module is a piece of code that can be dynamically loaded and unloaded from the Linux kernel. Writing a kernel module involves creating a source file, compiling it into an object file, and loading it into the kernel using `insmod` or `modprobe`.

A basic kernel module consists of two primary functions

1. init_module: The initialization function, which is executed when the module is loaded.

2. cleanup_module: The cleanup function, which is executed when the module is unloaded.

Here is an example of a simple "Hello, World!" kernel module

```c
#include <linux/module.h>

#include <linux/kernel.h>

#include <linux/init.h>

static int __init hello_init(void) {
```

```c
    printk(KERN_INFO "Hello, World! Kernel module loaded\n");

    return 0;

}


static void __exit hello_exit(void) {

    printk(KERN_INFO "Goodbye, World! Kernel module unloaded\n");

}


module_init(hello_init);

module_exit(hello_exit);


MODULE_LICENSE("GPL");

MODULE_AUTHOR("Author");

MODULE_DESCRIPTION("A simple Hello, World! Linux Kernel Module");
```
```

To compile the module, use the following Makefile
```

```makefile
obj-m += hello.o

all:

	make -C /lib/modules/$(shell uname -r)/build M=$(PWD) modules

clean:

	make -C /lib/modules/$(shell uname -r)/build M=$(PWD) clean
```

Once compiled, the module can be loaded with `insmod` and removed with `rmmod`

```bash
insmod hello.ko

rmmod hello
```

Writing Device Drivers

Device drivers are kernel modules that allow the operating system to interact with hardware devices. Writing a device driver requires interacting with the kernel's I/O subsystem, including handling interrupts, reading and writing to device registers, and managing buffers.

A simple character device driver consists of

- Open: A function that is called when a process opens a device file.

- Read: A function that is called when a process reads from a device file.

- Write: A function that is called when a process writes to a device file.

- Close: A function that is called when a process closes a device file.

Writing and debugging device drivers requires in-depth knowledge of hardware interaction and the Linux kernel's internal architecture.

Creating and Managing Shared Libraries

Shared libraries are a key feature of Linux and Unix-like operating systems. They allow code to be reused across multiple applications, reducing memory usage and ensuring that updates to the library are reflected across all applications that depend on it. Linux uses the ELF (Executable and Linkable Format) format for shared libraries.

Creating Shared Libraries

To create a shared library in Linux, the source code must be compiled with the `-fPIC` (Position Independent Code) flag, which ensures that the compiled code can be loaded into memory at any address.

For example, to compile a shared library

```bash
gcc -fPIC -shared -o libmylibrary.so mylibrary.c
```

This command creates a shared library named `libmylibrary.so`. The `-shared` flag instructs the compiler to produce a shared object.

Linking with Shared Libraries

When linking an application with a shared library, the linker searches for the library in standard directories (such as `/lib` and `/usr/lib`). You can specify additional directories using the `-L` option and the name of the library with the `-l` option.

```bash
```

```
gcc -o myapp myapp.c -L/path/to/library -lmylibrary
```

If the library is not in a standard location, you can specify the path using the `LD_LIBRARY_PATH` environment variable

```bash
export LD_LIBRARY_PATH=/path/to/library:$LD_LIBRARY_PATH
./myapp
```

Managing Shared Libraries

The ldconfig command is used to update the system's library cache, ensuring that shared libraries are available for dynamic linking.

```bash
sudo ldconfig
```

This command scans for shared libraries in standard directories and updates the cache located at `/etc/ld.so.cache`.

Network Protocols and Kernel Networking

Linux provides robust networking support, including a variety of network protocols, from TCP/IP to lower-level protocols like ARP and ICMP. Linux also provides kernel-level networking capabilities that enable efficient communication between processes on different systems.

Working with Network Protocols

Network protocols in Linux are implemented in the kernel and can be accessed via system calls or specialized libraries. Commonly used protocols like TCP and UDP are handled by the socket API, which allows processes to create network connections, send data, and listen for incoming packets.

To create a socket in Linux, you use the `socket()` system call

```c
int sockfd = socket(AF_INET, SOCK_STREAM, 0);
```

To send and receive data over a socket, you can use `send()` and `recv()` for connection-oriented communication (e.g., TCP) or `sendto()` and `recvfrom()` for connectionless communication (e.g., UDP).

Kernel Networking

Linux kernel networking is highly configurable and supports various protocols, such as TCP/IP, IPv6, UDP, and ARP. The kernel's networking stack handles the processing of packets, including routing, forwarding, and error checking.

To interface with kernel networking features, you can use tools like iptables for packet filtering and firewall management or netstat for displaying network connections and statistics.

Advanced Debugging Techniques

Debugging Linux applications requires a set of advanced techniques and tools. When working with low-level kernel modules or system-level programs, traditional debuggers like `gdb` might not suffice. Linux offers several tools to help with debugging, including kernel debugging, tracing, and performance analysis.

Kernel Debugging

To debug kernel code, you can use tools like KGDB (Kernel GNU Debugger) or KDB (Kernel Debugger), which allow you to set breakpoints and inspect kernel memory. KGDB is often used in conjunction with a serial console or Ethernet connection for remote debugging.

Tracing and Profiling

Linux provides powerful tracing and profiling tools, such as ftrace, perf,

Building and Deploying Linux Applications

Building and deploying Linux applications involves more than just writing code. It's about compiling your programs efficiently, preparing them to run on multiple platforms, packaging them for distribution, and automating the build process to ensure reliability and repeatability. Mastering these elements is essential for professional Linux software development, whether you're working on embedded systems, desktop applications, or server-side services. This section dives into compiler options and optimization, cross-compilation, software packaging, and build automation using Makefiles

Compiler Options and Optimization

When building Linux applications, the compiler plays a pivotal role. The GNU Compiler Collection (GCC) is the most commonly used compiler on Linux, and it offers a wealth of options to control the build process and optimize performance

Basic Compilation

At its most basic, compiling a C program with GCC looks like this

```bash
```

```
gcc hello.c -o hello
```

```
```

This compiles `hello.c` and outputs an executable called `hello`. But the real power of GCC lies in its compiler flags and options

Optimization Flags

Optimization flags in GCC help improve the performance or reduce the size of the final executable. These flags instruct the compiler to analyze and transform the code during compilation

- `-O0` disables optimization completely (default)

- `-O1`, `-O2`, and `-O3` progressively increase optimization levels

- `-Os` optimizes for size rather than speed

- `-Ofast` enables aggressive optimizations that may break strict compliance with language standards

Example

```bash
gcc -O2 myprogram.c -o myprogram
```

Debugging and Warnings

To aid in debugging and code quality

- `-g` includes debugging information for tools like gdb

- `-Wall` enables most common compiler warnings

- `-Werror` treats warnings as errors

- `-std=c99` or `-std=c11` specifies the language standard

Example

```bash
```

```
gcc -Wall -Werror -g -std=c11 myprogram.c -o myprogram
```

```
```

Using these flags helps prevent subtle bugs and improves maintainability

Cross-Compiling for Different Architectures

Cross-compiling is the process of building software on one platform to run on another. This is especially important when developing for embedded systems, ARM-based boards, or custom hardware

What You Need

To cross-compile, you need

- A cross-compiler toolchain for the target architecture (e.g., arm-linux-gnueabihf-gcc)

- The correct headers and libraries for the target system

- Configuration to inform your build tools of the new environment

Installing a Cross-Compiler

On Debian-based systems, you can install toolchains for various architectures

```bash
sudo apt install gcc-arm-linux-gnueabihf
```

Compiling with the Cross-Compiler

Once installed, use the appropriate compiler command

```bash
arm-linux-gnueabihf-gcc -o hello-arm hello.c
```

This produces a binary for ARM architecture. You can then transfer and run it on the target device

Managing Dependencies

For complex projects, you may also need to cross-compile libraries. Tools like `crosstool-ng` or build systems like `CMake` and `Autotools` can help manage this complexity

Packaging and Distributing Software (RPM, DEB)

After your application is built, the next step is distribution. On Linux, this usually means creating packages in formats like `.deb` (for Debian/Ubuntu) or `.rpm` (for Red Hat/Fedora). Packaging ensures your software installs cleanly, integrates with the system, and can be updated or removed easily

DEB Packages

Debian packages are built using tools like `dpkg-deb`, `dpkg`, and `debhelper`. A typical Debian package requires a specific directory structure

```plaintext

myapp/

├── DEBIAN

│   └── control

└── usr

    └── bin

        └── myapp

```

The `control` file contains metadata

```plaintext

Package: myapp

Version: 1.0

Section: base

Priority: optional

Architecture: amd64
```

Maintainer: Your Name <you@example.com>

Description: My simple Linux application

```

To build the package

```bash

dpkg-deb --build myapp

```

RPM Packages

RPM packages use spec files and tools like `rpmbuild`. A spec file defines how the package is built and installed

Example spec file

```plaintext

Name: myapp

Version: 1.0

Release: 1

Summary: My simple Linux app

License: GPL

Group: Development/Tools

BuildRoot: %{_tmppath}/%{name}-%{version}-root


%description

This is a simple application written for Linux systems


%files

/usr/bin/myapp

```
```

To build the RPM


```bash
```

```
rpmbuild -ba myapp.spec
```

```
```

Automating Builds with Makefiles

When your project grows beyond a few source files, manual compilation becomes cumbersome. Makefiles automate the build process using the `make` utility. A Makefile defines rules for how files are compiled and linked

Basic Makefile

```makefile
CC=gcc

CFLAGS=-Wall -O2

DEPS = mylib.h

OBJ = main.o mylib.o


%.o: %.c $(DEPS)

	$(CC) -c -o $@ $< $(CFLAGS)
```

myapp: $(OBJ)

  $(CC) -o $@ $^ $(CFLAGS)

```
```

In this example

- `CC` is the compiler

- `CFLAGS` sets compiler flags

- `DEPS` defines header file dependencies

- `%.o: %.c` is a pattern rule to compile object files

- `myapp` is the final executable target

Run `make` in the same directory to build your project

Clean Target

You can define a `clean` rule to remove compiled files

```makefile
clean:

    rm -f *.o myapp
```

Then run `make clean` to tidy your workspace

Advanced Makefile Features

Makefiles can also include conditional builds, multiple directories, and dynamic dependency generation. For large projects, tools like `CMake`, `Meson`, or `Autotools` can provide more sophisticated build configurations

Mastering the process of building and deploying Linux applications is key to creating reliable, portable, and maintainable software. Compiler optimization helps improve performance, cross-compiling extends your application's reach, packaging simplifies distribution, and Makefiles streamline the development process. Whether you're developing for desktop, server, or embedded environments, these skills form the foundation of professional Linux software engineering

Linux Programming Best Practices

Linux programming isn't just about writing code that works—it's about writing code that's maintainable, efficient, secure, and easy for others to understand and improve. Whether you're contributing to an open-source project or developing a proprietary application, following best practices ensures your software is robust and respected in the development community. This chapter covers key principles including code style and documentation, error handling and logging, performance tuning, testing and continuous integration, and collaborating within the open-source ecosystem

Code Style and Documentation

Consistent code style makes your code readable and maintainable, especially in team environments or open-source projects

Use a Consistent Formatting Style

Pick a coding style and stick with it. For C programming in Linux, the Linux kernel style is often used. Some key conventions include

- Indent with tabs (not spaces)
- Place braces on the same line for control structures

- Limit lines to 80 characters

- Use descriptive variable and function names

Example


```c
if (count > 0) {
    process_items(count);
}
```


Use tools like `clang-format` or `astyle` to automatically enforce your style guide

Write Meaningful Comments

Comment your code to explain why something is done—not just what it does. Avoid redundant comments and focus on complex logic or decisions


```c
/* Retry if the resource is temporarily unavailable */
while (retry_count < MAX_RETRIES && errno == EAGAIN) {
    retry_count++;
    // Attempt to acquire the resource again
}
```


Document APIs and Functions

Use tools like `Doxygen` or plain markdown to document functions, structures, and modules. Clearly define parameters, return values, and side effects

```c
/**
 * add_user - Adds a new user to the system
 * @name: the name of the user
 * @uid: user ID
 *
 * Returns 0 on success, or a negative error code on failure
 */
int add_user(const char *name, int uid);
```

Good documentation acts as a guide for new contributors and helps future you understand past decisions

Error Handling and Logging

Ignoring or improperly handling errors is one of the fastest ways to introduce bugs and instability into Linux applications

Check Return Values

Always check the return values of system calls and library functions. For example, `malloc`, `open`, `read`, `write`, and `fork` can all fail

```c
int fd = open("data.txt", O_RDONLY);
if (fd == -1) {
    perror("Failed to open file");
    exit(EXIT_FAILURE);
}
```

Use errno and perror

Linux system calls set the global `errno` variable when errors occur. Use `perror` or `strerror` to print meaningful error messages

```c
if (write(fd, buffer, len) == -1) {
    fprintf(stderr, "Write failed: %s\n", strerror(errno));
}
```

Logging

Logging is essential for debugging, monitoring, and auditing. Use different log levels (info, warning, error, debug) and consider using syslog or libraries like `log4c`

```c
syslog(LOG_ERR, "Service failed to start: %s", strerror(errno));
```

Don't log sensitive information like passwords or API keys. Secure logs by setting appropriate file permissions

Performance and Efficiency

Efficient code is important for responsiveness, scalability, and resource conservation, especially in constrained environments

Avoid Unnecessary Memory Allocation

Minimize dynamic memory allocation, especially in loops or high-frequency code paths. Reuse memory or use stack allocation when possible

Profile Your Code

Use tools like `gprof`, `perf`, `valgrind`, and `strace` to identify bottlenecks and inefficiencies

```bash
valgrind --tool=callgrind ./myprogram
```

Use Efficient Data Structures

Choose data structures that match your needs. A hash table is better than a list for frequent lookups. Use libraries like `glib` for robust implementations

Optimize I/O

Batch I/O operations when possible. Avoid frequent small writes to disk or the network. Use memory-mapped files (`mmap`) for large file operations

Testing and Continuous Integration

Testing ensures your software behaves correctly and reliably across environments and over time

Unit and Integration Tests

Write unit tests for individual functions and integration tests for full workflows. Use testing frameworks like `cmocka`, `check`, or `Google Test` for C/C++

```c
assert(add_user("alice", 1001) == 0);
```

Automate your tests using `Makefile` targets or scripts

Continuous Integration

Set up CI pipelines to automatically build and test your code whenever changes are pushed. Tools like GitHub Actions, GitLab CI/CD, Jenkins, or Travis CI are widely used

CI ensures that new code doesn't break existing functionality and enforces coding standards across contributors

Static and Dynamic Analysis

Use static analysis tools like `cppcheck` or `clang-analyzer` to catch bugs early. Use `valgrind` to find memory leaks and undefined behavior at runtime

Open Source Contribution and Collaboration

Linux thrives on open-source collaboration. Whether you're submitting patches to the kernel or building your own tools, understanding community norms is key

Learn the Workflow

Most open-source Linux projects use Git. Learn how to fork, branch, commit with clear messages, and create pull requests or patches

```bash
git checkout -b feature-improve-logging
```

Commit messages should be short but descriptive

```plaintext
Improve error logging for socket failures
```

Follow Contribution Guidelines

Always read a project's `CONTRIBUTING.md` file. Follow their coding style, test your changes, and write meaningful commit messages

Participate in Code Reviews

Be open to feedback and participate in code reviews respectfully. Review other people's code as well—it's a great way to learn and give back

Respect Licensing

Understand open-source licenses like GPL, MIT, Apache, and BSD. Respect them when using or sharing code

By adopting these Linux programming best practices, you ensure that your code is clean, secure, and scalable. Whether you're working solo or as part of a massive open-source project, these principles help you write software that's not just functional—but dependable, maintainable, and future-proof

Case Studies and Real-World Examples

Understanding Linux programming theory is essential, but applying it to real-world projects is where your skills are truly tested and refined. Real-world case studies not only reinforce what you've learned—they expose the practical challenges, performance bottlenecks, and architectural decisions that shape robust Linux software. In this chapter, we'll explore four case studies: developing a networked application, building a Linux system service, writing a command-line utility, and optimizing a Linux-based application. Each example will walk through the objectives, technical considerations, implementation strategies, and lessons learned

Developing a Networked Application

Creating a networked application involves multiple layers of the Linux stack—sockets, I/O, concurrency, and error handling. Let's look at a simple TCP client-server application that transfers messages between two systems on a local network

Objective

Build a TCP chat server that handles multiple clients and echoes back messages. The server must handle concurrency efficiently and remain responsive

Key Components

- Socket programming (AF_INET, SOCK_STREAM)
- Select or multithreading for concurrency
- Message formatting and parsing
- Graceful shutdown handling

Implementation Overview

- The server creates a socket, binds it to a port, and listens for incoming connections
- It uses `select()` to handle multiple clients without threading or forks
- Each message from a client is echoed back, and the server maintains a list of active connections

```c
fd_set master_set, read_fds;
FD_ZERO(&master_set);
FD_SET(server_fd, &master_set);

while (1) {
    read_fds = master_set;
    select(fdmax+1, &read_fds, NULL, NULL, NULL);

    for (int i = 0; i <= fdmax; i++) {
        if (FD_ISSET(i, &read_fds)) {
            if (i == server_fd) {
                int newfd = accept(server_fd, NULL, NULL);
```

```
        FD_SET(newfd, &master_set);
        if (newfd > fdmax) fdmax = newfd;
    } else {
        int nbytes = recv(i, buf, sizeof buf, 0);
        if (nbytes <= 0) {
            close(i);
            FD_CLR(i, &master_set);
        } else {
            send(i, buf, nbytes, 0);
        }
    }
}
}
}
```

Lessons Learned

- `select()` is effective for managing small-scale concurrency, but for high performance or many connections, `epoll` or threading may be better
- Error handling (timeouts, disconnections) must be robust to avoid server crashes
- Logging is critical during debugging and scaling

Building a Linux System Service

System services are background processes (daemons) that start with the OS and perform long-running tasks. This example demonstrates building a custom service to monitor disk usage and write logs

Objective

Create a system daemon that periodically checks disk usage on mounted volumes and logs usage stats every 10 minutes

Key Components

- Daemonization using `fork`, `setsid`, and `chdir`
- Logging with `syslog`
- Systemd integration with a service unit file
- File I/O and `/proc` or `df` command parsing

Implementation Strategy

1. Daemonize the process

```c
pid_t pid = fork();
if (pid < 0) exit(EXIT_FAILURE);
if (pid > 0) exit(EXIT_SUCCESS);
```

```
setsid();
chdir("/");
umask(0);
```

2. In the daemon loop, collect and log disk usage

```c
while (1) {
    system("df -h >> /var/log/disk_monitor.log");
    sleep(600);
}
```

3. Create a systemd unit file `/etc/systemd/system/disk-monitor.service`

```ini
[Unit]
Description=Disk Monitor Service

[Service]
ExecStart=/usr/local/bin/disk-monitor
Restart=on-failure

[Install]
WantedBy=multi-user.target
```

```
```

4. Reload systemd and start the service

```bash
sudo systemctl daemon-reexec
sudo systemctl enable --now disk-monitor.service
```

Lessons Learned

- Daemons should handle signals (SIGTERM) gracefully for clean shutdowns
- Systemd provides powerful service management, including auto-restarts, logging, and dependency handling
- Logging to files or using syslog helps in diagnosing issues post-deployment

Writing a Command-Line Utility

Command-line tools are essential in Linux. Writing a well-structured, feature-rich CLI tool involves parsing arguments, handling file I/O, and providing clear output

Objective

Develop a utility named `finddup` that scans a directory tree and reports duplicate files based on content hash

Key Components

- Recursive file traversal using `opendir` and `readdir`

- SHA-256 hashing for content comparison

- Use of hash maps to track duplicates

- Command-line parsing with `getopt_long`

Implementation Strategy

- Traverse the file system and generate a SHA-256 hash for each file
- Store hashes in a hashmap; if a hash repeats, print the path as a duplicate

```c
unsigned char hash[SHA256_DIGEST_LENGTH];
SHA256_CTX sha256;
SHA256_Init(&sha256);
while ((bytes = fread(buf, 1, sizeof(buf), file)) != 0)
  SHA256_Update(&sha256, buf, bytes);
SHA256_Final(hash, &sha256);
```

- Use `getopt` to support flags like `--path`, `--min-size`, `--verbose`

```c
while ((opt = getopt(argc, argv, "p:s:v")) != -1) {
  switch (opt) {
    case 'p': path = optarg; break;
```

```
        case 's': min_size = atoi(optarg); break;
        case 'v': verbose = 1; break;
    }
}
```
```

Lessons Learned

- Using libraries like OpenSSL simplifies cryptographic tasks like hashing
- Efficient memory and error handling are critical for tools that work on large file sets
- Clear usage help (`--help`) improves user experience

# Optimizing a Linux-Based Application

Optimization often begins when performance issues appear in real-world usage. This case study involves profiling and optimizing a high-load log parser

## Objective

Improve the performance of a multi-threaded application that parses massive log files in real-time and writes summaries to disk

## Key Issues
- High CPU usage
- Memory fragmentation and leaks
```

- Slow I/O performance on spinning disks

Optimization Strategy

1. Profile the application with `perf` and `valgrind`

```bash
perf record ./logparser
valgrind --leak-check=full ./logparser
```

2. Identified that a custom string splitting function was inefficient and had memory leaks. Replaced with a pooled memory allocator and optimized logic

3. Switched from `fprintf` to `write` and batched disk writes

```c
write(fd, buffer, total_size);
```

4. Reused thread-local buffers to avoid repeated allocations

5. Improved concurrency with lock-free queues and minimized use of mutexes in the hot path

Results

- CPU usage dropped by 40%
- Memory consumption stabilized with no leaks
- Throughput increased by 3x on the same hardware

Lessons Learned

- Small code inefficiencies multiply under load—profiling is non-negotiable
- System calls like `write` and `mmap` are faster than standard library functions in high-performance contexts
- Threading and memory management must be tuned together for optimal results

These real-world case studies illustrate how Linux programming concepts translate into practical solutions. From building system daemons to writing efficient CLI tools, each scenario shows the importance of architecture, performance tuning, security, and maintainability. Working through such examples not only solidifies your skills—it prepares you for the complex, fast-moving world of Linux software development

Resources for Further Learning

Linux programming is a vast and ever-evolving domain, and while mastering the fundamentals is a significant achievement, the real journey begins with continuous learning. The Linux ecosystem is supported by a strong community, countless open-source projects, comprehensive documentation, and events around the globe that foster collaboration and discovery. This chapter highlights some of the best ways to continue developing your skills and staying current with the latest in Linux programming. Whether you're seeking reference books, interactive communities, advanced tools, or in-person experiences, there's a wealth of knowledge available to support your growth

Linux Programming Resources and Books

Books remain one of the most reliable ways to gain deep understanding, often structured to take you from beginner to advanced levels. Here are some of the most respected and widely used Linux programming resources

The Linux Programming Interface by Michael Kerrisk

This book is considered the gold standard. It covers system calls, processes, threads, signals, file I/O, and everything in between. Its thorough explanations and practical examples make it essential reading

Advanced Programming in the UNIX Environment by W. Richard Stevens

Though focused on UNIX, this book has tremendous relevance to Linux. It dives into system-level programming and covers the nuts and bolts of process control, file systems, and signal handling

Linux System Programming by Robert Love

This concise and accessible book offers a focused look at system-level programming for Linux. Topics include files, memory, processes, and system calls. It's ideal for those looking for a practical and readable companion

How Linux Works by Brian Ward

This book is perfect for those wanting to understand how Linux operates under the hood. It doesn't just teach commands—it explains the design decisions behind them

The Art of UNIX Programming by Eric S. Raymond

This is more philosophical and design-oriented. It explores the UNIX programming mindset and is a fantastic read for understanding the broader cultural and technical influences behind Linux

Online Communities and Forums

Online communities are one of the most powerful tools available to Linux developers. These platforms provide real-time help, exposure to new tools and techniques, and the opportunity to contribute and receive feedback

Stack Overflow

With thousands of Linux-related questions and answers, Stack Overflow is a great place to search for solutions to programming issues. Be sure to ask well-formed questions to receive the best responses

Reddit

Subreddits like r/linux, r/linuxquestions, and r/linux4noobs are full of active users sharing ideas, troubleshooting issues, and discussing news. r/unixporn is popular for system customization inspiration

LinuxQuestions.org

One of the oldest Linux help forums. It's well organized and welcoming to new users. It covers everything from installation to kernel development

GitHub and GitLab

Not just for code hosting—these platforms are vibrant ecosystems of open-source collaboration. You can learn by reading the code of well-established projects, submitting issues, and contributing pull requests

Discord and IRC

Many Linux communities and distributions maintain real-time chat channels. Look for official channels for Arch, Ubuntu, Fedora, and kernel development. These are great for live problem-solving and meeting other developers

Advanced Tools and Libraries

Mastering the right tools is crucial for writing better, faster, and more secure Linux applications. Here are some advanced tools and libraries that will enhance your development workflow

strace and ltrace

These tools trace system calls and library calls, respectively. They are indispensable for debugging issues in compiled programs

perf and gprof

Use these tools for profiling and performance analysis. perf is powerful for CPU-bound tasks and kernel performance tuning

Valgrind

A suite of tools for memory debugging, memory leak detection, and profiling. Especially useful for C and C++ programs

GDB

The GNU Debugger is an essential tool for stepping through code, analyzing crashes, and inspecting program state at runtime

libevent and libuv

These libraries abstract away platform-specific I/O and concurrency, helping you build scalable network applications

Boost C++ Libraries

If you're working in C++, Boost offers a vast set of portable and high-performance libraries, many of which work seamlessly in Linux environments

ncurses

For terminal-based interfaces, ncurses allows you to create dynamic, interactive applications right in the console

Clang Static Analyzer and cppcheck

Static analysis tools that help find bugs without running your code. They are excellent for code quality and safety

Conferences and Workshops

Attending Linux and open-source conferences is one of the best ways to stay current, connect with peers, and gain insights directly from experts. Whether virtual or in-person, these events offer talks, workshops, and networking opportunities

Linux Plumbers Conference

Focused on the core infrastructure of Linux, this event attracts maintainers, kernel developers, and advanced users who work on performance, boot processes, and system services

Open Source Summit by the Linux Foundation

This global event brings together developers, architects, and community leaders from across the open-source ecosystem. It covers everything from security and development to legal and governance issues

FOSDEM (Free and Open Source Developers' European Meeting)

Held in Brussels each year, FOSDEM is one of the most popular free and community-driven conferences in the open-source world

All Things Open

A large open-source conference based in the US, featuring sessions on Linux programming, DevOps, AI, and more

Local Linux User Groups (LUGs)

These community groups host regular meetups, workshops, and hackathons. They're great for beginners and professionals alike to share knowledge in a friendly environment

Workshops and Bootcamps

Organizations like the Linux Foundation, Udemy, Coursera, and EdX offer intensive training sessions on everything from Linux fundamentals to kernel development and embedded systems

Whether you're debugging kernel modules, building microservices, or contributing to open-source tools, continuing education is essential in the Linux world. From legendary books and hands-on forums to specialized tools and global conferences, the Linux ecosystem is rich with opportunities to grow. The key is to stay curious, keep building, and never stop exploring.

Appendices

The appendices serve as quick-access resources and practical guides that complement the main chapters of this Linux programming handbook. These sections are designed to support your journey from beginner to advanced developer, offering handy reference material and setup instructions to help streamline your work. Whether you're searching for a command you've forgotten, a specific system call, or step-by-step help setting up a development environment, the appendices are your go-to section for practical support

A Linux Command Reference

This section offers a curated list of essential Linux commands that programmers and developers frequently use. While Linux has thousands of utilities, the commands below form the core toolkit for system-level development, navigation, and debugging

File and Directory Management

- `ls` – List directory contents
- `cd` – Change directory
- `pwd` – Show current directory path
- `cp`, `mv`, `rm` – Copy, move, and delete files
- `mkdir`, `rmdir` – Create and remove directories

- `find` – Search for files in a directory hierarchy
- `du`, `df` – Disk usage and space info

File Viewing and Editing

- `cat`, `less`, `more` – View contents of files
- `nano`, `vim`, `emacs` – Text editors for quick edits or code development
- `head`, `tail` – Display the start or end of a file

User and Permission Management

- `chmod`, `chown` – Change file permissions and ownership
- `whoami`, `id`, `groups` – Display user identity
- `sudo`, `su` – Run commands as another user, typically root

Process and System Monitoring

- `ps`, `top`, `htop` – View running processes
- `kill`, `killall` – Terminate processes
- `nice`, `renice` – Set or change process priority
- `uptime`, `free`, `vmstat` – View system resource usage

Networking Tools

- `ping`, `traceroute`, `netstat`, `ss` – Diagnose network issues
- `ifconfig`, `ip`, `nmcli` – Configure and display network interfaces
- `curl`, `wget` – Fetch data from remote servers

Package Management (Varies by Distribution)

- `apt`, `dpkg` – Debian-based systems (Ubuntu, etc.)
- `yum`, `dnf`, `rpm` – Red Hat-based systems
- `pacman` – Arch Linux

Development Tools

- `gcc`, `g++` – GNU C and C++ compilers
- `make` – Automate builds using Makefiles
- `gdb` – GNU Debugger
- `strace`, `ltrace` – Trace system and library calls
- `valgrind` – Detect memory errors

B Common System Calls and Functions

System calls form the bridge between your program and the Linux kernel. These low-level operations let your code perform tasks like file access, process management, and memory allocation. Below are commonly used system calls and standard library functions in Linux programming

File I/O System Calls

- `open()` – Open or create a file
- `read()` – Read data from a file descriptor

- `write()` – Write data to a file descriptor
- `close()` – Close an open file descriptor
- `lseek()` – Move the read/write pointer
- `stat()`, `fstat()` – Retrieve file metadata

Process and Thread Management

- `fork()` – Create a new process
- `exec()` family – Replace process image
- `wait()`, `waitpid()` – Wait for process termination
- `getpid()`, `getppid()` – Get process and parent process IDs
- `pthread_create()`, `pthread_join()` – Create and manage threads

Memory Management

- `malloc()`, `free()` – Dynamic memory allocation
- `mmap()` – Map files or devices into memory
- `brk()`/`sbrk()` – Legacy memory allocation methods
- `munmap()` – Unmap memory regions

Signals

- `signal()`, `sigaction()` – Set up signal handlers
- `kill()` – Send signals to processes
- `alarm()`, `sleep()` – Timer-related functions

File and Directory Operations

- `mkdir()`, `rmdir()` – Create and remove directories
- `unlink()` – Remove a file
- `rename()` – Change file or directory name
- `chmod()`, `chown()` – Modify file permissions and ownership

Networking

- `socket()` – Create a socket
- `bind()` – Assign an address to a socket
- `listen()` – Mark socket as passive for incoming connections
- `accept()` – Accept incoming connection
- `connect()` – Establish connection
- `send()`, `recv()` – Send and receive data

C Linux Programming Environment Setup

To begin Linux development, you'll need to set up a capable environment. This section walks through the steps for configuring your Linux system, installing essential development tools, and tuning your workspace for efficient coding

Choosing a Linux Distribution

While any distribution can support development, some are more developer-friendly:

- **Ubuntu** – Great for beginners, wide community support, easy to install packages
- **Fedora** – Bleeding-edge tools and GNOME integration
- **Debian** – Stable and reliable, often used for servers
- **Arch Linux** – Customizable and lightweight, great for experienced users
- **Pop!_OS** – Built for developers and engineers with out-of-the-box tools

Essential Packages

Make sure you install the base development tools. On Ubuntu/Debian:

```bash
sudo apt update
sudo apt install build-essential manpages-dev gdb valgrind git
```

Other useful packages:

- `vim`, `emacs`, or `code` for editing
- `make`, `cmake` for building
- `strace`, `ltrace` for tracing
- `perf` for performance monitoring

Editor and IDE Setup

Choose the editor that fits your workflow:

- **Vim or Emacs** – Lightweight and powerful, ideal for working within terminals
- **VS Code** – Rich plugin support, debugger integration, and language server support
- **CLion** – Advanced C/C++ IDE with powerful analysis tools
- **Geany or Kate** – Lightweight graphical editors for GTK environments

Debugging and Profiling Tools

- `gdb` – Essential for stepping through programs
- `valgrind` – Useful for catching memory leaks
- `perf` and `gprof` – For analyzing performance bottlenecks

Version Control Setup

Use Git to manage source code and collaborate

```bash
sudo apt install git
git config --global user.name "Your Name"
git config --global user.email "you@example.com"
```

Platforms like GitHub and GitLab are useful for hosting and collaborating on open-source projects

D Index

The index is an alphabetical listing of terms, commands, functions, and key concepts covered throughout this handbook. It helps you quickly locate topics or tools when you're troubleshooting or revisiting specific sections

Examples of what you might find in the index:

- alarm function usage

- bash scripting best practices

- chmod command

- errno variable explanation

- fork and exec examples

- gdb debugging steps

- memory leak detection

- pthread_create syntax

- select function usage

- valgrind output interpretation

The index will be auto-generated at the back of the print or digital version of the book. Be sure to refer to it whenever you need a quick lookup or refresher

The appendices serve as your daily desk companion—whether you're diving into a new project, refreshing your memory on a system call, or looking for ways to fine-tune your Linux development environment. With these tools and references at your side, you'll be well-equipped to tackle the challenges of Linux programming with confidence and clarity

www.ingramcontent.com/pod-product-compliance
Lightning Source LLC
LaVergne TN
LVHW060122070326
832902LV00019B/3090